Recovery From Loss
A Personalized Guide
To The Grieving Process

Lewis Tagliaferre
Gary L. Harbaugh, Ph.D.

Health Communications, Inc.
Deerfield Beach, Florida

Library of Congress Cataloging-in-Publication Data

Tagliaferre, Lewis
    Recovery From Loss : A Personalized Guide To The Grieving
Process / by Lewis Tagliaferre and Gary L. Harbaugh.
        p.   cm.
    Includes bibliographical references.
    ISBN 1-55874-073-2
        1. Grief. 2. Bereavement—Psychological aspects. 3. Death—
    Psychological aspects. 4. Widows—Psychology. 5. Widow-
    ers—Psychology. I. Harbaugh, Gary L.   II. Title.
    BF575.G7T34   1990   89-48223
    155.9'37—dc20   CIP

©1990 Lewis Tagliaferre and Gary L. Harbaugh
ISBN 1-55874-073-2

Publisher: Health Communications, Inc.
        3201 S.W. 15th Street
        Deerfield Beach, Florida 33442

Contents

Preface

This book has grown out of my own grief work that resulted from the untimely death of my wife, Rosalene, at 7:21 p.m. on Tuesday, September 3, 1985, after 31 years and 20 days of a traditional, loving, interdependent marriage that began on a hot Saturday afternoon on August 14, 1954. The trauma, suffering and psychic pain I encountered drove me to a study of the reactions people experience upon the premature death of their spouse and how people cope with the inevitable readjustment. This is my interpretation of what I have learned through my own process toward survival. It is a continuing process, one that I do not expect will ever be completely finished because the past is a permanent part of me, as it is of you. In a real way, this is my memorial gift to Rosalene and our two children, Sharilyn and Noel. Of necessity, it is written from a surviving husband's point of view, which few other writers have taken. But I hope it will be helpful to surviving spouses of both sexes.

The contribution to this work made by Dr. Gary Harbaugh is greatly appreciated. I am grateful for his support, friendship, love and the professional edge his insights and clinical experience provide. His review and the integration of his innovative work on personality and loss raises this book above the level of personal therapy. I wish also to thank all those members of the Widowed Persons Service of Northern Virginia and other friends who helped me to test out these ideas in the real world of bereavement.

The books Dr. Harbaugh and I found to be the most helpful are listed in the references and we recommend them to you for further reading. The references listed in them will lead you in turn to countless others, so there is no shortage of resources to help you continue your search if you so choose. Wherever concepts are expressed from the work of these authors, identification of the source is included.

I have tried to communicate my empathy for all those who grieve the loss of their spouse with the personal pronoun "I." I know what it is like because I walk in your shoes. *To highlight my more personal reflections, they are printed in italics.* The rest of the text combines my real-life experience with the clinical experience of Dr. Harbaugh. Although this is not a perfect means of integrating the separate contributions we both have made, it seems to be the most efficient.

We believe this is a powerful contribution to the support of those who suffer this pinnacle of loss. I hope you find reading it as helpful as preparing it was to me.

Lewis Tagliaferre

Recovery From Loss is concerned with you as a whole person. As you read this book you will see that many resources are available to those who grieve and some of them are very good. But we want to offer something more — a new perspective that combines personal experience with a special way of understanding how to manage grief. In a remarkable, intensely personal, yet appealing and non-threatening way, Lewis Tagliaferre shares in this book his experience with untimely grief. Drawing on his experience is our way of pointing out that everyone who experiences the loss of a loved one is an individual with unique and personal needs. However, what you read is based on more than Lew's personal experience. What we offer also rests on extensive and solid research.

There are many who have contributed to our understanding of grief and to the preparation of this book. My wife, Marlene, has lived with grief and has offered valuable insights into the family dynamics that are involved, especially in co-dependent families. In addition, Lew and I are both appreciative of the editing gifts of Marie Stilkind and Kathleen Fox, the clerical support of Kay Haddox, Jill Szturm, Kathy Nodo and Loxi Dailey, and the collegial support of Dr. Mary H. McCaulley, president of CAPT, Dr. Naomi L. Quenk, past president of APT, Dr. Allen Hammer and Lorin Letendre of Consulting Psychologists Press.

When it comes to grief theory, you will find us quick to acknowledge the contributions of those who preceded us. We have made extensive notations of the work of others both in the text and in the bibliography.

However, *Recovery From Loss* also breaks new ground. Over the past 20 years I have developed a holistic understanding of personhood which I interrelated with the insights of my former teacher, Dr. Elisabeth Kubler-Ross, pioneering author of *On Death and Dying*. Since 1980, I have been integrating my earlier studies with the Myers-Briggs theory of psychological types. To my work, Lewis Tagliaferre has insightfully added the dimension of William Worden's model of adaptation to loss which he identified as: (1) to accept the reality of the loss, (2) to experience the pain of grief, (3) to adjust to an environment in which the deceased is missing and (4) to withdraw emotional energy and reinvest it in new relationships. He has also tapped into Kubler-Ross' "quadrants of energy," i.e. physical, intellectual, emotional and spiritual, in a most powerful way. When our combined model is applied to the loss experience of the widow and widower, grief in midlife is seen from a new perspective. We hope our way of looking at grief will help you understand better the thoughts and feelings that most grieving persons have — whether that person is yourself or someone you love. Even more, we hope our work will encourage you and give you a lively sense of hope.

If you are grieving the death of a husband or wife or if you have lost a spouse and realize there is unfinished business with that loss, this book is for you. Read it, use it and pass it along with our blessing and best wishes for a better tomorrow.

Gary L. Harbaugh, Ph.D.

I see the moon,
The moon sees me,
The moon sees somebody
I'd like to see.
God bless the moon,
God bless me,
And God bless somebody
I'd like to see.

Introduction

Every year there are over two million funerals in the United States. About 800,000 of them leave grieving spouses behind. Since about one-third of all deaths occur under the age of 65, many spouses are faced with what we call "untimely grief." However, even if death comes at a relatively mature age, many survivors still feel cheated. Gone are the years together. Gone are the years ahead and the future activities they had hoped for. Grief can be devastating. Grief is all the more difficult if it is complicated by unresolved issues, as often occurs in dysfunctional families.

If you are grieving the loss of a loved one right now, it is important that you realize grief is a normal reaction to loss. We grieve because we value that which was lost. Our grief may be even more intense if we perceive that we have very little social support during this time or that control of our lives has been stripped from us. Feeling totally alone and completely abandoned is not an unusual reaction to monumental loss. Friends and family often encourage grievers to go on as though nothing has happened. To please them you may be tempted to suppress your feelings and your thoughts but this reaction can prevent the healing process and delay the pain that signals healing.

When you carry unhealed emotional wounds around with you like extra baggage, you actually prolong the period of recovery. Unfortunately, feelings of disorganization, panic, guilt, anger, loneliness and anxiety are all normal parts of the grieving process. Reconstruction does not occur all at once. It can be a long and painful process.

Grief is not classified as a mental illness. Although the strength of your reaction may cause you to *fear* the loss of your sanity, there usually is nothing like that to fear. If you do not have other complicating mental problems, grief can be and usually is eventually managed successfully through adaptation to your new lifestyle, difficult and painful as the process may be.

Reaction through grief to the loss of your spouse is a process, not an event. It is not something you get well from as you do a cold or even a serious illness. It is an irrevocable part of you. You can feel better but you will be different from now on. No one else can ever replace the one you lost in your life. You may find another who may become your companion, friend, lover or spouse, but it will be a different relationship from the one you have permanently lost. So this is not a book to read quickly and store away. It is a living document that can guide you through your process for as many years as you want to use it.

While the pain and suffering of the grief experience is great, it is reassuring to know that people do usually survive the loss of a loved one and eventually reconstruct a new life. Not only that, but people are often able to grow through the grief experience, sometimes to the point of being able to help others who suffer similar experiences. Both loss and growth are painful processes. This book is intended to pass along some of what the grief experience teaches about both.

The intensity of the reactions and feelings that swamped me after the initial shock of watching my beloved wife die was something I hardly expected. As she had predicted to one of her friends, I was a "basket case." When my grief became more than I could handle alone, I entered grief counseling and therapy, consulted psychics, joined support groups and took the prescribed medication for sleeplessness and depression to get me through the numb, numberless days. I drove myself through the daily chores of work and life somehow. I was driven to learn all that I could about what was happening to me, so I began researching bereavement. My study of grief, death, mourning, etc. also led me to a study of life, its purpose and meaning, its conflicts and paradoxes. It is said that when a student is ready, a teacher will be provided. So I searched for information that might help me understand what was happening to me because I feared total loss of my mind, my job and even my physical survival. During the very deepest, blackest days, I contemplated suicide. It was through this searching process and my struggle for survival that the idea for this book and my relationship with Dr. Gary Harbaugh were born.

Many books have been written about grief and bereavement and more are published every year. There are, of course, many religious perspectives that have been offered over the centuries. However, most of the literature written by psychologists and psychiatrists concerning grief is much more recent. Although Sigmund Freud wrote *Mourning and Melancholia*, published in 1917, little additional work on grief was produced until research by Dr. Erich Lindemann in 1944 marked the beginning of modern studies of reactions to death. He studied survivors of nearly 500 people who died in Boston during a fire at the Coconut Grove nightclub in the fall of 1942. He found that grief produces some typical responses that affect the ability of surviving family members to function as they had before the tragedy. Lindemann's contribution was to describe the normal grief responses as well as indicators of a grief survivor's need for special help.

Individual professionals, agencies, institutions and even the federal government have looked into the problems of the bereaved. Society as a whole is affected not only by the loss of the individual who dies but also by the diminished contributions of the close survivors if their grief is not resolved in such a way as to enable them to re-enter productive life. Books and research studies, support groups, counseling and psychotherapy are all efforts to help people manage their grief. And they can help — especially when they show sensitivity to the particular pain and suffering that comes with the loss of a spouse.

Grief resulting from death of a spouse can also raise spiritual questions for survivors. Religious literature says a lot about grief because much of a clergyperson's work is to help people through times of loss. A major loss challenges the grieving person to deal with the mystery of spiritual matters because the loss must somehow be integrated into a survivor's approach to spirituality. This is not easy for many people. For some, it demands a reassessment of their entire belief system.

Although I thought I was fairly well educated and grounded in religious faith, I found that I was just a beginner on the road to spiritual becoming. We are all learners on the pathway we call life. And as we learn, then perhaps we will have something to teach. Perhaps now is the time and place for you to take another step in the direction of your personal "becoming." If so, you may find spiritual help in this book. If it is not yet your time for applying this material to your life situation, then perhaps you might just save it for a time when you feel ready to take the next step.

Death and the grief that follows require us to probe the deeper mysteries of life that death raises in our minds. It causes us to ask the ultimate questions. There are many ways to respond to these questions, and we shall try to suggest some of the variety of spiritual responses. However, please remember that each person is unique. People have different personalities, values, family and cultural backgrounds, educational training and life experiences. You will need to adapt our ideas to your own situation in your own way and in your own time. It is important to give yourself permission to grieve in your own way, at your own pace, even though some of your friends, co-workers or even your close family members may not be able to understand. They will each have their own pathway to travel, even if they were close to your spouse, because their relationship with that loved one was different from yours. Only you had the unique relationship with your spouse that is experienced through the intimate context of marriage.

In past times the reality that a survivor was going through a grief process was highlighted by certain rituals. For example, a wreath was placed on the front door or a black arm band or black clothing might be worn for a certain period of time.

I did those things. Some people may have thought I was strange, I suppose, but I wanted the whole world to know what happened to me and why I looked and acted the ghastly way I did. I wanted the world to stop a moment and take note of the severe loss that it had so nonchalantly discarded.

Some cultures still have a prescribed period of public mourning and a ritual for survivors to follow. In our society few of these rituals remain. Consequently, others may not be as considerate of you as you would like them to be during this time. They may actually expect you to wear a mask of normality in public to protect them from their own horror at the contemplation of death.

Our society as a whole tends to be death-denying. In 1969 Elisabeth Kubler-Ross sensitively broke into the taboo surrounding death with the publication of *On Death and Dying.* But many people continue to deny their mortality. As Rollo May said so well, we have made death obscene, unmentionable, even pornographic. It may be the last great taboo of this society. Old people are put away in nursing homes — "out of sight, out of mind." We pretend our own mortality is off in some infinite future.

Paradoxically, although modern medical technology can prolong death long past the time of unaided existence, our society is less equipped to deal with death than were our ancestors who lived with it more openly. Our youth-oriented society keeps at arm's length those who remind us we are mortal. Our mobility often means that nuclear families are cut off from close relatives during times of terminal illness and loss. Not too long ago families usually consisted of three generations living in close proximity. Death was a fact of everyday life. Now families are usually separated by distance and life among relatives is not so well integrated. There is little experience with death in normal life.

Perhaps we work so hard to prolong life artificially in order to compensate for the guilt of living so separately. One usually un-planned but definite implication of such separations is that it is possible for many to limit their contact with death and grieving family members to the few days surrounding a funeral.

While the hospice movement is trying to bring us back into touch with our humanity and what we have to offer each other during the final stages of life, the majority of Westerners still seem to want to keep as much distance as possible between themselves and death, as well as from the disabling bereavement that follows. Except for small-print obituaries stuck away in newspapers or the occasional eulogy to a deceased public celebrity, leaders of our public media have refused to present mortality as it really is and we have bought the illusion they present to us.

The consequence of keeping death at a distance means that we are all the more unprepared to deal with grief. We are not at all prepared for the devastation the loss of a spouse brings to the survivor. We are compelled to cope with our loss without having family role models or having learned appropriate coping strategies from society.

Even our religious institutions may not always deal well with the fact of mortality. That is especially true when a loss occurs out of what we consider to be the normal order in the stream of life. *When we do not find the solace we were expecting to find in our faith, the weight of grief is even heavier.* We can feel cut off from the religious community, cut off from a resource we may always have felt would be there for us if we really needed it. When an expected source of help does not come through, our sense of loss increases greatly.

Of course, the feeling of loss and the degree of our need for support is in part related to the nature of the loss. Some losses seem to be harder to deal with than others. When the loss is by death, we may manage pretty well the death of a co-worker, a relative, perhaps even our parents. But when our spouse dies, we may find little comfort from any quarter. After the funeral is over, we can be left pretty much alone, feeling forsaken even by family and friends, to work out our protest, deprivation and adjustment for ourselves. No one seems to know how to help us. Professionals may seem only to attend to our symptoms. People who have not walked in our path-way seem unable to understand us or to help us unless they have had specific training in counseling bereaved spouses. "Life must go on," that most awful of trite platitudes, is thrust upon us figuratively if not literally by well-meaning friends and relatives at a time when we might rather just die ourselves.

The loss may feel like an amputation. It is obvious that someone who has lost an arm or a leg is disabled and most rational people will make allowances for that condition. But since the psychic wound of our grief is not visible like an amputation or paralysis or other physical trauma, we are given too little time and too little sympathy from established institutions. Heart-attack victims and surgical pa-tients may be given several weeks or months by employers to recover, but mourners are expected to be at work and back on the go in a week or so. Some find help from support groups and professionals in social work, psychology and psychiatry but in the end, we ourselves must find our way through the maze and out into the light of day again. It is a lonely, frustrating, lengthy, expensive and energy-consuming process.

The shock of untimely grief can cause great confusion as you try to sort out the many unexpected physical and emotional symptoms. You become extremely vulnerable to suggestions from well-meaning friends and relatives. You hardly know what to do as you stumble along from hour to hour, day to day, submerged in the ocean of bereavement. I felt totally out of control for the first time in my life and the feeling of par.ic terrified me. What I needed was a model, road map or pathway through the maze. I needed something to put some control back into my life.

Although each of us brings a unique background of experience, beliefs and personality to the work of untimely grief, we believe you can be helped by putting some structure to the process. Many writers have chosen a series of phases or serial modules to describe the process of loss, shock, protest, disorganization and reorganization of life that we call grief.

Kubler-Ross described stages in her patients' experiences of terminal illness: the stages of shock, denial, anger, bargaining, depression and then, hopefully, not resignation but acceptance. Gary Harbaugh has compared Kubler-Ross's stages with the research of John Bowlby, Erich Lindemann, Granger Westberg and C. Murray Parkes, who also believed that grief is a process. More recently, Stephen Gullo and Connie Church, John James and Frank Cherry, and Verena Kast have suggested sequential models of the grief work required after the loss of a love. These models are certainly useful and we recommend them as very helpful aids, especially if they are used in association with what we present in this book. Our work takes a somewhat different and, we think, more powerful approach to recovering from the grief caused by the loss of a beloved spouse.

We think *grief calls us to pay attention to ourselves as whole persons.* In *A Model for Caring,* Dr. Harbaugh presented the various stage theories in relation to a holistic model that drew on the American Medical Association's categories of the physical, mental, emotional and social dimensions of life. Then, in *The Faith-Hardy Christian,* he showed how each of these dimensions is integrated spiritually. More recently, Harbaugh combined his holistic model and the work of Kubler-Ross with the Myers-Briggs Type Indicator to show how different personalities handle various kinds of loss situations.

In this book, we extend and deepen Harbaugh's model by integrating it into the grief tasks of William Worden and relating them to Kubler-Ross's insights into the physical, intellectual, emotional and spiritual resources available to persons in grief. As a combined effort, this new Harbaugh-Tagliaferre model brings together our concern to understand the grieving person as a whole person who has a unique personality and personal values that will affect how the grief is resolved.

The integrated approach we present in this book is our contribution to all of you who suffer this life-changing process of recovery from the untimely loss of your spouse. We hope it will also be helpful to volunteer support leaders and professionals who counsel with bereaved spouses. The loss of control that comes with bereavement is immensely stressful and can cause harmful biochemical changes in the brain, affecting even our resistance to disease. Emotionally, when we feel out of control, a feeling of anxious helplessness can set in. The model of grief presented in this book may help you to put some confidence back into your life, thereby improving your outlook and potential for future happiness and contentment. Our work is just a beginning but we hope it will be a helpful beginning.

We recognize that different people have their own approach to learning and dealing with crisis, so this structured approach may not be the best for you. But since it puts together elements of many different approaches and structures them into a logical framework, you may find it a useful piece to your puzzle. Indeed, the basic premise of the model we present is that *grief is a unique experience* for each survivor, based on your personality as well as many other circumstances in your particular situation.

Descriptions of isolated steps in the process of others, syrupy poems about the sweetness of bereavement and other such attempts at comfort did not help me all that much in finding my own pathway. Instead, such illustrations got in the way of my own grief work. Untimely grief is not just a bitter pill to swallow, it is a galling banquet that you are forced to digest one course at a time. You can only tolerate it in small bites.

We want to talk to you in these pages as we would talk to you in person. To make this dialogue more real, we have at certain places left space for you to insert your own name or that of your spouse. Please begin now.

Write your first name on this line: _____ and share with us in this process of discovery and renewal. You will also see spaces designated for inserting the name of your spouse (or the loved one you have lost) as follows: *(D for Deceased)* D _____. You may find this difficult to do at times, but our experience indicates you will find it may help you face more fully the fact of your loss. We hope you will take the opportunity to enter this more personal dialogue with us as we accompany you on your journey to reconstruction.

Difficult as it is to accept, grief work is accomplished only while we are in pain and suffering. It may be tempting to stay in the numbing state of shock and denial to avoid the wave of suffering that emerges as we begin to face our new reality. But according to Helen Keller, who was born blind and deaf and suffered greatly for many years before a miracle of love helped her live a full life, "The best way out is always through."

You can choose to accept the pain of grief or the pain of suppress-ing grief. Since grief is a gift to help you live through your loss naturally, suppressing it is ultimately far more painful than accepting it. We are conditioned by modern medicine to escape the discomfort that comes with illness. Even terminal illness and dying can be expe-rienced relatively free from pain through modern anesthetics and pain-controlling drugs. Not so with grief. Although some phsyicians are quick to prescribe tranquilizers and other pain-avoiding measures, many professionals now believe such intrusions only complicate the grief process unless they are needed for purely medical reasons. Some medications to aid sleep or induce rest may be desirable for a brief time. Most researchers agree, however, that trying to avoid the suffering of grief may cause you more lengthy, severe reactions than leaning into the feelings and letting yourself experience them fully.

Unfortunately people in our culture frequently are not equipped to understand what you are going through unless they have expe-rienced it themselves. So managing your grief while continuing to function in polite society will create severe stress on you. We hope this book will help make it more tolerable.

One more thing, (your name) _____. Your *progress through grief is not a linear one with steps or phases neatly following one after the other.* Although a book is a linear device with pages following one after the other, the plan we have outlined does not require that you use it that way. You can select sections at random as they seem to meet your needs. We do suggest that you read the book from front to back one time. After that, you will be able to refer to specific sections that apply and provide support where you are in your grief process. Sometimes you will be able to identify a specific numbered section that meets your present needs. Other times it may seem that so many things are happening to you at once you will not be able to select a single section for comfort. At such times just let things rest for a day or so. After that you may be able to sort out your feelings enough to make another attempt.

The important thing is to keep on searching for the pathway
that produces the healing you need. The process is not easy or
quick. Each survivor has grief feelings that must be worked
through in one way or another and as completely as possible for
reconstruction as a whole person to be effective. The process of
recovery from grief can be likened to moving a certain volume of
water through a pipe. If the pipe is larger, the time it takes is
shorter than if the pipe is smaller but with a larger pipe, the flow
is much faster and can be overwhelming.

The deeper your attachment to D _____ and
the more intertwined your lifestyle was, the harder you will be hit by
the loss. In order to emerge on the other side as a new whole healed
person, you will have to let yourself experience "the 20 steps of grief."

1

20 Steps Of Grief

One of the best known measures of stress, the Holmes-Rahe Social Readjustment Rating Scale, ranks the loss of a spouse by death as more stressful than any other life-changing event. Compared with the 100 stress points given the death of a spouse, the second most stressful life change, divorce, was rated at 73. Of course, not everyone reacts in the same way when a spouse dies. Death comes at different times of life and each couple has a different life situation and a unique relationship. However, the untimely death of your spouse has to be one of the most stressful changes you will ever experience. Your spouse was probably the most important person in your life, possibly for many years. You may not remember much of your single life before you were married. Now you must live with this loss or die in the attempt. It is not one you can walk away from.

And that is your problem. Of all the five-plus billions of people on the earth, this loss is uniquely yours. No one but you had that relationship with *D* _____, your spouse, and no one but you can know your grief as you experience it.

Only you have those memories of the times, good and bad, for better or worse, in sickness and in health, for richer or poorer, till death did you part, that you spent together with *D* _____. You can't have surgery to cut those memories out of your head and you can't remove them any other way without destroying your mental health. Others who have not suffered such a loss can scarcely relate to you now. You may have faced other losses and changes in your married life together: loss of job, health, possessions, parents, relatives, children, etc., but now you must face this one alone. How you deal with it and your changing relationships with family and friends are partly related to your overall approach to change, so let's explore that subject for just a moment.

Change

Even though it is a universal experience, most people do not like change. They have a limited capacity to accept it. People actually fear change that exceeds their limits of tolerance because it is a threat to their basic security needs. We do experience some life changes that can bring benefits, such as the thrill of driving a new car, moving to a new house or taking a new job. But it is fearful when change means you have to give up something of value for uncertainty. Some people spend more energy resisting change than they do adapting to it. Because it is the most stressful of changes, the loss of a spouse causes the strongest grieving reactions.

Grief may cause us to conduct painful self-examination, to look inside ourselves. To look at ourselves through the eyes of reality is not easy. It causes suffering in proportion to the intensity of our feelings about the loss. Grief also causes an unequalled emptiness and sense of longing. Sadness is a new part of you now. It permeates your entire being, even to your bones and spirit.

Your world is not as it was before. Things are not and cannot ever again be as they were. To go on, you have to let go and turn loose of a comfortable past. Grief requires that you file yesterday away and look forward to tomorrow. Grief demands growth and there can be no growth without suffering. It is a law of life. You are in a new

room of life, a frightening room, a lonely room, all by yourself. To
fear grief is to be normal.

Dealing With Change

Growing through untimely grief depends upon four main ideas
about change that come from psychologist Dr. Richard Flint:

1. The loss of your spouse is more than the loss of a relationship.
It may be the loss of a complete way of life. If your past seems more
secure and peaceful than your present or your future, you may want
to go back to your yesterday with D _____ and
live there. There is a secure haven in the past because you can make
it what you want it to be in your fantasies. But change wants to
make sure you do not get lost in the memory of yesterday. Change
wants to point you to tomorrow even though all you may see is a
maze of frustration, despair, worry and fantasies. You must learn
this: People who live in yesterday have no today and destroy any
possibility of tomorrow. The choice is yours. There is help, but you
must walk through this transition by yourself.

2. Every change brings with it a painful ending. You cannot
experience a beginning until you have had an ending. Marriage is
the end of singleness. Birth is the end of pregnancy. Death is the
end of physical life. The end of mourning is when you let go of
yesterday with your D _____. You realize you
cannot go back, but you may rebel against your own knowledge to
avoid the pain of adjustment. So long as you hang onto what was,
you will never discover what can be. You are not who you
were, _____. Neither is your spouse,
D _____. You are part of a transition, both
yours and your spouse's. For that transition to be growth for both
of you, you must file yesterday away in the file of experience,
accept today as you are and see tomorrow as your new adventure.
You want to hang on because endings are fearful. Endings mean
finality. We resist finality, but an ending actually is the beginning
of new growth to make room for the blessings in front of you.
Without accepting the ending, growth would be denied and there
would be only frustration at having to live with a situation you
cannot control. But we would rather not have growth if it means
painful change, so it is forced upon us. And it is painful. You must
learn how to channel this energy into a positive outcome. New
beginnings are scary, but now you must move on to discover the
new whole you.

3. Some part of you will resist growth because change is always frightening. Change can make you feel lost, disoriented, alone, unprepared and scared for a much longer time than you expected. It puts you at war with yourself. That war will remain inside you until it is fought and won. The symptoms and signs of the struggle may include worry, stress, anxiety, fear, despair, panic, depression and woe for longer than you expected or your friends and relatives will easily tolerate.

4. It is through the process of change that reconstruction of life begins. Reconstruction of your life will demand all the courage you have. *Courage is the taking of action in spite of fear.* Some marital changes may be chosen voluntarily, but neither of you chose for D _____ to die. Your grief caused by the loss of D _____ may not ever be completely gone. The pain will lessen and become tolerable, but it has now become a part of you. You will never be the same person again. You alone will know the difference.

Choosing life when you feel like dying is not easy but it is the only answer. You may feel it would be easier to just end it all. There is a way through grief, although it may not seem possible right now. What is needed is courage to face the demands of life, even when those demands seem overwhelming. Courage may sometimes falter but we believe there is a Higher Power that helps us face fear and despair. While it may not seem so at times, you have been given all the resources you need. The rest of this book will help you identify those resources and learn to use them.

I refused to accept the idea that my grief was a growth experience. How could such a devastating experience produce growth when all I could see was despair and suffering? Looking back at my progress so far, I can see that growth has indeed occurred. Maybe it was undesired, maybe it was in a direction that surprised me and maybe I could just as well have done without it, but the process of life does go on until it stops. And you have the choice to use your grief for growth or to let it choke off your development toward becoming a more wholly integrated person.

If our marriage is blessed with health and happiness, we can deny the reality of death for many years, and we usually do. We are politely sympathetic to others who walk this path before us and we avoid the brutal, insulting confrontation until it is our time. We may know intellectually that one of us may have to watch the other one die but we do not really internalize that fact. It is a defense mechanism that permits us to enjoy life with our loved ones.

The untimely death of a spouse cuts through our denial. Whether young, middle-aged or old by current medical standards, we all have a time to die. Medicine can prolong life in some cases but eventually death comes. If *D* _____ had a lengthy illness, you may have had time to do some preparatory grieving, but you still may not have internalized the fact of death. If the event was more sudden, violent, physically destructive or unexpected, the process of detachment and reconstruction may be longer and more difficult.

First Reaction: Shock

When the event of death strikes its way through to your conscious mind, the first reaction may be a defensive numbness or shock as you try to avoid the intense pain of loss. You may not feel much of any emotion for a while, just a feeling of being disconnected from your world. You may drift like an astronaut who is circling the earth outside of his space vehicle, untethered to all his familiar sources of life. You also may feel as if all your insides have been ripped out and replaced with cotton stuffing. When the shock does wear off, it can be replaced with intense pain and suffering so striking as to cause you concern for your own physical and mental well-being. This second wave of remorse, longing and sadness is something few can understand if they have not actually experienced it.

You suffer because a material and spiritual part of you has been amputated unwillingly. It may be as though a Siamese twin part of you has been wrenched away without the benefit of surgery, leaving a gaping, hemorrhaging wound in your chest. Your physical survival is threatened. Your condition may be so devastating at first that words cannot describe it or convey your feelings to others.

For more than a year a red rash appeared in the center of my chest, just over my heart. I often felt connected to Rosalene by the feeling of a spear driven through my heart, binding me to her. I wanted to tell everybody how I felt but it takes so many words that even close friends are bored with the endless repetition. They just don't want to share in that pain. I felt completely isolated in my private mourning. There was no comfort anywhere as I searched in vain for a place I belonged, where I would feel whole again. If you are like me, you may feel there is no such place.

State Of Suspension

After the initial numbing shock wears off, you are then buffeted by so many different feelings of such unexpected, uncontrollable intensity that you cannot think clearly. That makes you afraid — afraid of losing your job if you are still working, possibly afraid of losing even your sanity. You may not be able to sleep or you may want to sleep all the time. You may eat too much or not want to eat at all, gaining or losing weight. Food often just sticks in your throat with no taste at all. You may feel uncontrollable emotions of rage, anger, jealousy of healthy couples, fear, guilt, despair, panic and depression. You may have no motivation to continue even the most routine tasks of life.

I stopped balancing my checkbook, and I did not wash the dishes until the sink was full or take out the garbage until the wastebasket was overflowing.

Your job, your relations with family and friends, your very social being are put into a state of suspension that you may not ever have experienced before. In turn, this loss of control can send you into a panic if it seems your own life is being threatened. And always there is the unrelenting sadness and self-pity.

Physical Imbalance

You may feel sexually impotent. You may be tempted to do some foolish things in your frantic search for healing, such as jumping into bed with the first person who invites you, spending outlandish amounts of money on irrational purchases, running around the world taking trips or searching for your lost spouse in crowded shopping centers. You may actually experience symptoms of the same illness your spouse died of. And you may get sick. You may consciously want to die. Many diseases seem to be related to physical imbalances that can be caused by the distress of grief 18 to 36 months later. C. Murray Parkes and others indicate that widowers die at a higher rate than do widows or married men in the same age groups. Mortality rates for unmarried widowers do not return to levels comparable to married men until nine years have passed.

Medical research is proving that the mind does indeed exert great control over the body. Through chemical neurotransmitters, signals are sent from the brain to all the glands that produce hormones which control our immunity to disease. When we sense lack of control or insufficient social support, these signals are changed. This allows the many foreign agents that always occupy our bodies to act against the body in ways we are able to successfully resist under normal conditions. In the uncontrollable situation of loss, we can neither fight nor flee, which are the usual responses to crises. We must learn to flow with the change if we are to sustain mental and physical health.

Withdrawal

After a few weeks or months of concern, your still-coupled friends and even your relatives may stop bringing you food or inviting you out to eat or for entertainment, worship, etc. Some of your closest friends do not know how to deal with you, so they probably don't bother at all.

Many times people, in their feelings of inadequacy and helplessness, walk away to avoid their own pain of watching you suffer. You may realize that most of them were your spouse's friends and not really your own if your spouse was the social planner of your marriage.

You soon feel unwanted, with a diminished sense of self-worth. You are no longer married but you are not yet single. You don't feel as if you belong anyplace. Your personal sense of identity is threatened. If the terminal illness of your spouse was gradual, you may have withdrawn from active social life without realizing it.

Life will seem unreal for a long time when compared with your happy, contented past. That feeling will last far longer than you probably expected, maybe over two or three years, with the unexpected length of it also causing you further distress.

Surviving the loss of your spouse is the greatest challenge of your life. It will test every concept you possess about the meaning of life, belief in God, relationships, family, love, work and the cosmos. It will test every instinct for survival you possess. Successful reconstruction of your life will demand great strength. The line separating normal from abnormal reactions to the loss of your spouse can be so close to mental illness it is horrifying to confront. You try to avoid that confrontation but you can't.

You may also begin a search of reading material for help as I did. One resource can lead to another and another. While all of these resources provided some help, I found that none of them contained all of the answers I was seeking. It is like putting together a jigsaw picture puzzle without the picture. You may find some of the pieces fitting together on a random basis, but without the big picture on

*the box, it is practically impossible to see how they all fit together. You
search and search among the pieces for a fit, only to be frustrated
in failure again and again.*

You may find that this discussion has been too emotional for you.
It may be forcing you to confront feelings that you have been
suppressing because you fear the pain is too great to face. That may
be a necessary form of defense for you right now. If that is your
situation, it is okay to put this book away for a while, perhaps a
month or more, and return to it later when you are ready. As time
passes you may feel better able to deal with those feelings. Time by
itself is not necessarily a healer if you do not work through your
grief. You must work with grief at the pace only you can tell is
correct. Each of us must take as much time as we need to assimilate
the acute changes that grief brings. Don't berate yourself because
you seem to lose progress at certain times. This, too, is normal.
Give yourself permission to recover at your own pace, in your own
style. You are unique, and your grief is unique.

Grief Structure

When you are ready to do constructive grief work, you may need
some structure, a road map or model to lead you along the way.
Without structure you won't be able to track your progress, which
is very important to some people. If you cannot sense progress,
feelings of frustration and futility may be added to your discomfort.
As we mentioned in the introduction, most counselors and writers
seem to prefer a staged or phased approach to discussing and
managing the grief process. Elisabeth Kubler-Ross suggested that
terminally ill patients seem to experience stages of denial, anger,
bargaining and depression before they reach a constructive stage of
acceptance. This approach has proved to be very useful in helping
terminally ill patients and their families live until they die. Other
writers have adapted the phased or staged model, with some variations, to the grieving process.

While stage models are useful, we suggest an alternative model that
we have found to be even more helpful. This is important because
people do not walk, crawl or claw (nobody successfully runs) through
grief in neatly staged, sequential phases with clear beginnings and
endings. We tend to jump around in a random fashion, working on
various aspects as they need to be handled at the time.

Sometimes we must tackle more than one task at a time. And we
bring a variety of personal resources from our training and experi-

ence to each task of grief. So any useful model needs to provide the flexibility needed by a wide variety of unique people in unique circumstances and be applicable to their unique situations.

Rather than take a phased or staged approach to grief, we have found the tasks of grieving as derived from the work of William Worden to be most useful in understanding the process. We have modified his model somewhat to reflect the experiences that seem to be more universal among grieving spouses. With this modification, we find five specific tasks to be managed in grief. These are:

1. To acknowledge
2. To feel
3. To substitute
4. To detach
5. To reconstruct

To these tasks we bring the entire inventory of our being. These amount to physical, intellectual, emotional and spiritual resources. Each of these is applied in unique ways to each of the five tasks on a schedule that is tailored to each mourner. By combining the tasks with these resources, we have constructed the following model of grief work. As with any model of the real world, this one is probably not a perfect replication of your experience. We have found, applying it to other survivors in group settings, that it seems to meet the needs of many in a variety of ways. In the chapters to follow, we will refer to each task and resource separately. To conveniently identify the steps, each one is simply labeled with a number, 1 to 20. That will make it easier to walk together through the process of grief. Table 1.1 illustrates this new model of grief work.

Table 1.1 — The 20 Steps Of Grief

Resources	Tasks				
	Acknowledge	Feel	Substitute	Detach	Reconstruct
Physical	1	5	9	13	17
Intellectual	2	6	10	14	18
Emotional	3	7	11	15	19
Spiritual	4	8	12	16	20

The general tasks of grief — to acknowledge, to feel, to substitute, to detach and to reconstruct — are fairly easy to describe, although they may be extremely difficult and painful to carry out. They are not necessarily conducted in the order from left to right as shown in the figure. You may find yourself working on all of them simultaneously or concentrating on one or more of them as you feel the need. With time, however, we do tend to move from left to right in the process of grief work. Again, it is important to understand that this process usually takes more time than most people expect. It can be two or three years or even longer before you feel that reconstruction is well along.

Some widows and widowers remarry in a year or so after the loss of their spouses. Many of these quick marriages end in early divorces, possibly because they are mistaken attempts at substitution rather than the culmination of healthy reconstruction. You should try to put off any such action, including selling your house and relocating, for at least one year. It may take longer if you are not yet fully in control of your rational thinking processes. Such changes only pile additional stress on top of the stress of grief.

Five Tasks Of Grief

1. **To ACKNOWLEDGE** means to reluctantly own, internalize or admit that D _____ is dead. It means to overcome denial of the horrible fact that D _____ is no longer alive or available to you in a physical sense. Denial is okay for a time as a defense mechanism but you cannot stay in denial and maintain your mental health.

2. **To FEEL** means to experience all the results of the loss of D _____ in your life. These feelings include emotions of fear, anger, guilt, panic, jealousy, depression and even love, in addition to many physical symptoms. It may be the most frightening task to accomplish. The feelings can be so terrifying that you want to be freed of them immediately but suppression or denial of them is not healthy.

3. **To SUBSTITUTE** means to find ways of replacing all the functions you need in your life that D _____ filled for you. You may find that you really can live without some of the roles D _____ provided. Deprivation of the more significant roles may drive you to seek satisfaction

through replacement. Managing this task is crucial to successful recovery.

4. To **DETACH** means to disconnect, disengage, unfasten or
separate yourself and your emotional attachment from
D _____. You must consciously change
your commitment in order to be free to invest in new relationships. Before you can make healthy new attachments,
you must release your emotional investment in the past.

5. To **RECONSTRUCT** means to construct again, to rebuild, to
make over a new, integrated life from the remaining parts of
your old life. You may not want to reconstruct for some time
but the alternative of refusing to undertake this task may cause
you even more suffering.

The *resources* that you bring to these tasks involve your entire
being. In Western cultures we are oriented to sensory, material
awareness of the body, mind and emotions through daily life experiences. Religious views usually affirm these categories but also add
spirit or soul. Looking at a body in a casket or on a deathbed sets
your mind to wondering about the essence of life. Death injects the
mystery of life into our thinking and forces us to grapple with the
unknown and unknowable.

We have chosen the physical, intellectual, emotional and spiritual as the four resources or aspects of the self in our model.
These four seem to be implied in the Old Testament scriptures
(Deuteronomy 6:5) and were reinforced by Jesus as the first great
commandment: "You shall love the Lord your God with all your
heart, and with all your *soul,* and with all your *strength,* and with
all your *mind"* (Mark 12:29ff.; Luke 10:27). As we will show later,
they also relate very closely to a model of personality that is
rapidly gaining acceptance.

Physical, Intellectual And Emotional Resources

Strength seems to us to relate to the *physical* body and its
ability to do work. It also involves the world of the physical
senses: feel, touch, smell, hear, weigh, measure, see, etc. *Mind* is
the *intellectual* ability to think rationally, to absorb information,
make decisions and reason logically. From this energy, we learn
most of our cultural skills, values and lifestyles. *Heart* relates to
the *emotions* of fear, anger, guilt, jealousy, depression and love.
Soul is the essence of humanity that finds expression in various
forms of spirituality.

Spiritual Resources

In the Old Testament, "soul" is the translation of the Hebrew word "nephesh" which really stands for the whole person. In the New Testament, it is the Greek word "psyche" that is usually translated as "soul." Sometimes the word "spirit" is used to point to humans as more than creatures of the flesh.

The soul or spirit, therefore, points to a deeper reality in personhood that includes a concept of God or, if you prefer, a Higher Power. Because of its intuitive, mystical, mysterious aspects and because our culture emphasizes logical, sensory behavior, the concept of soul or spirit is not explored much in secular Western writing.

As a matter of fact, schools of psychology and psychiatry and most writers on grief do relatively little with the spiritual. However, *we believe confronting death raises spiritual questions,* even if they are unrecognized or called by another name. True healing requires that we work through the spiritual implications of our loss. What is more, a spiritual perspective brings another set of resources into our management of untimely grief. For these reasons, we'll now look at some alternative ways people have drawn upon spiritual resources in their recovery from grief. Even if you do not consider yourself a religious person, we hope you will carefully read this subsection and reserve your judgment until after you complete it.

I had an intellectual and maybe even emotional awareness of religion, as many people do. I had taken a few college courses in philosophy and religion and I was a professing Christian, but the look on my Rosalene's face as she sighed those last few breaths and sank into the pillow confronted me with a shock I had not expected. I watched and felt her body — the body I had loved and adored so intimately — turn grayish blue, rigid and cold. The transition from animate to inanimate dredged up ancient questions about the relationship of matter to energy and death to life that I had to deal with. This incredible experience afflicted me with the symptoms of post-trauma shock for a long time.

Humans have been searching since the beginning of recorded time for answers to the meaning of life and the meaning of death. Greek metaphysics and entire religious belief systems were developed to offer possible explanations and interpretations. Our Western contemporary society is not metaphysically oriented. At times the inappropriate behavior of a few religious leaders so sours people on institutional religion that some feel cut off from the kinds of re-sources that have traditionally provided support during times of loss.

The topic of spirituality can be a problem for those who demand laboratory proof for all they believe. Until the time comes when scientists can weigh, measure, feel, touch or otherwise scientifically observe the nonmaterial aspect of being human, some will doubt the existence of anything beyond what can be comprehended by the physical senses. In our review of the alternative ways that people have tapped into spiritual resources, we'll see that sometimes there is an effort to link science with spirituality. After looking at those paths, we want to discuss a more traditional religious approach.

Combining Science And Spirituality

Modern psychiatry is beginning to combine the physiology of the brain, the science of the mind, and the philosphy of the ages in new and wonderful ways to help us understand our behavior. Elisabeth Kubler-Ross, Blair Justice, Raymond Moody, Kenneth Ring, Bernie Siegel and a few others have taken a view that people are composed of energy in various forms. We are familiar with physical energy, but a growing body of research points to the presence of intellectual, emotional and spiritual energy as well. Furthermore, some of this energy is directed by subconscious or unconscious forces beyond the control of the intellect.

The first law of thermodynamics in physics states that energy can neither be created nor destroyed, only transformed from one form into another. A person is, therefore, energy in mass. Einstein pro-posed in his famous law of matter that $E = MC^2$. His formula means that energy is equal to the mass times the speed of light squared. In other words, energy and mass are related in terms of speed. If mass can be speeded up to the speed of light (roughly 186,000 miles per second) squared, it can be converted into pure energy. Although no one has yet been able to accelerate mass to these exotic speeds, when the mass of heavy atoms is accelerated, great amounts of energy are released.

Dr. Kubler-Ross, who has become internationally known, has confounded some of her medical peers with the revelation that she had an experience in which she sensed a speeding up of the molecules of her body that pushed her through a traumatic shock barrier until she emerged in a state of total peace and resonance with the universe. This kind of experience bears some resem-blance to what Moody and Ring have reported. They evaluated thousands of reports from people all over the world who described near-death experiences. A similar transition through trauma to peace was a common event among them. Did Einstein intuitively define a basic truth about the cosmos in his famous formula, or does there just appear to be a connection?

Einstein's theory forms the basis not only for the atom and hydrogen bombs, but also for nuclear fusion and fission in the production of electricity. Researchers are now reporting many exciting new findings about how the brain uses electrical and chemical energy to control the life forces of the body. It seems that how we think does indeed have a great deal to do with how we feel. It may affect whether we get sick or not. Through the creation of special chemical substances called neurotransmitters, the brain seems to control the immune system through the endocrine and hormonal glands. These, in turn, secrete substances that fight off diseases. According to Justice and Siegel, many of these control substances have now been isolated and identified down to the molecular level. What is intriguing is the unknown mechanism by which the brain is "instructed" to create these control substances. The link between the mind and the brain is inferred, but not yet fully understood.

Modern psychology includes a belief by a growing number in the presence of an inner self that transcends the conscious and unconscious minds. If we can tap this resource, we obtain power over our physical circumstance. People who have overcome severe handicaps and risen through crises often attribute their behavior to awareness and mobilization of this Higher Power. It has been related to miraculous healing, financial and personal success and enhanced human relationships. Such experiences are sometimes attributed to use of human intuition, i.e. the ability to "know" without sensing. It is said that we all have this ability but few of us have learned how to use it. This power within is unleashed by expression of nonjudgmental unconditional love for others and all elements of life on earth. It is as though consciously deciding to exhibit the good in our makeup drives out the bad in our lives and opens our environment to potentially unlimited peace of mind and happiness. Contact with this Higher Power can be experienced through meditation, positive image visualization, prayer and other means.

In light of all this research, it is understandable that some might propose to expand the scientific study to include the transition from life to death and beyond, a hypothesized transition from physical energy into spiritual energy. More attention is being paid to developing laboratory methods that will enable scientists to investigate more fully what happens at death. Until recently, such inquiries have been the province, not of science, but of metaphysics.

Metaphysical Alternative

The "scientific" approach has a lot in common with metaphysical alternatives to the problem of life and death. Deriving from ancient Greek and Egyptian thinkers and promoted by Eastern mystics, metaphysics seeks to explain the relationship between matter and energy by logic and philosophy in ways that do not require scientific verification. Sometimes people search in these directions when their religious supports break down.

In my period of deepest distress after losing D Rosalene, I searched for support and comfort among my church family and found none to be of help. The additional shock of this turn in events led me to search beyond Western religion and I began a study of other worldwide spiritual beliefs. I began to fear that I couldn't survive if I did not find an answer to the unanswerable questions that were driving me on a personal quest for understanding. I began a continuing investigation of the life-death dilemma, one that continues and probably will continue until my own day of passing finally settles the mystery.

People in all cultures seem to have a need to believe that life exists beyond death in some form, that the separation from loved ones is not permanent. Some people even claim to have perception or powers of understanding that enables them to establish a link between this world and a world beyond. That such a link is possible seems to be based on a view of death as the liberation of spiritual energy or soul from the physical body. According to this view, at death the energy of the soul is released from its confinement in time and space and leaves the body as a butterfly emerges from a cocoon. This release may be associated with breathing, the last breath being the departure from physical life. It is only the body, however, that dies. The soul or spirit lives on.

This way of thinking is compatible with the "near-death" research of Ring and Moody. Thousands of out-of-body "after-death" experiences have been documented from around the world, proving for some that consciousness and identity exist after the physical body has been declared dead. There is a remarkable similarity between these accounts reported by a variety of people in wide-ranging cultures. Some see this as the coming together of scientific and metaphysical views in a new theory of the mystery of life and death.

Reincarnation Theory

In addition to the possibility of communication between those who continue to live in this world and those who have "passed on," some Eastern views suggest a cycle of death and rebirth (reincarnation) wherein there is the opportunity to grow over the course of several lifetimes toward a higher level of awareness and perfection.

Sometimes added to the theory of migration of souls is a belief in a kind of predestination or fate, called *Karma*. In this theory, each sojourn on earth is carefully planned before physical birth, even to the selection of culture and parents who will provide the learning experience that is needed. Death is also a preplanned event. Thus, there are no accidental departures and each one is perfectly timed and conducted, no matter what the chosen time or form of exit. One does not leave until one's work is completed, but does not stay one second longer. The cause of death, whether natural, accidental, suicide or homicide, is merely the final phase of completion of our work.

Another theory is that those who have died relate to people in this life as a kind of spiritual guide.

In looking at spirituality and death from a variety of perspectives, we ranged considerably beyond what would be generally accepted within many religious traditions. If you are interested in looking further at the contemporary effort to bridge the gap between scientific, metaphysical and religious points of view, you may want to read *Beyond the Gates of Death* by Hans Schwarz.

Religious Perspectives

This section is titled Religious Perspectives rather than *The* Religious Perspective because among the world religions and even within a single religion such as Christianity, there are a wide variety of beliefs.

Virtually all religions bring a deeper awareness of the meaning of life and most of them offer a way of looking at death. Muslims believe that after death there is a day of judgment for all individuals. Those within Islam are spared from the wrath of Allah. Buddhists do not focus on the individual surviving death because the goal of life is to grow spiritually beyond attachments to material life and beyond an orientation to self.

Some religions stress that there is a continuing relationship of those who die with those who live. The Chinese reverence of ancestors is based on a sense of the continuity of the past with the present, a continuity that imposes specific obligations on the part of those who remain.

A Jewish Perspective

The Jewish understanding of death is related to the understanding of personhood that comes out of Hebrew anthropology. The ancient people of Israel understood themselves to be whole persons before God and they saw life as relationship. Shalom actually is impossible to experience apart from a right relationship with oneself, with others and with God. Something of this faith comes through the following meditation shared by a caring Jewish friend from the "Gates of Prayer" (the *New Union Prayer Book*):

How Can I Understand Death?

What can we know of death, we who cannot understand life? We study the seed and the cell but the power deep within them will always elude us.
Though we cannot understand, we can accept life as the gift of God.
Yet death, life's twin, we face with fear.
But why be afraid? Death is a haven to the weary, a relief for the sorely afflicted. We are safe in death as in life. There is no pain in death. There is only the pain of the living as they recall shared loves and as they themselves fear to die.
Calm us, Oh Lord, when we cry out in our fear and our grief.
Turn us anew toward life and the world. Awaken us to the warmth of human love that speaks to us of You.
We shall fear no evil as we affirm Your Kingdom of Life.

In this meditation, both life and death are presented in the context of a relationship with God. The appeal is to the Lord of Life who gives courage to face even the fact of death. The focus, however, remains on life rather than on death.

A Christian Perspective

As Gary Harbaugh has pointed out earlier in *The Faith-Hardy Christian*, the Christian way of looking at personhood is based on the Hebrew anthropology that Jesus himself accepted as true. A person must be understood as a whole person before God, apart from which there is no peace (Shalom). There is a wide range of understanding among Christians not so much about what life is but about how to live it. Death also is subject to many interpretations, including a great number of views on exactly what happens at the moment of death and what becomes of the person after death.

Even with all these variations, there are some convictions that Christians seem to share. Among them are:

1. *A hope.* Christians are hopeful in the face of death, which is possible because that hope is grounded in the grace of God rather than on anything that a person does (or fails to do). Death, for Christians, is not the end. Passages from the New Testament speak of life that transcends death: "He that believes in me though he were dead, yet shall he live" (John 11:25). Christians believe that the God who has upheld them in life is also present and caring in the hour of death, not only for them but also for those who are left behind.

2. *A victory.* Death cannot hold the Christian because the Christian believes that the power of God is stronger than death. The Christian believes that what the Bible refers to as the "sting" of death is overcome by the victory given by God through the death and resurrection of God's son, Jesus Christ. Death was swallowed up in the victory of his resurrection.

3. *A promise.* God's promise is that those who die in the Lord have a place in God's Kingdom. Some Christians believe that it is a personal place — "I go to prepare a place for you" (John 14:2) — and a happy place — "And God will wipe away every tear from their eyes" (Revelation 7:17). A bereaved Christian spouse and family is comforted by believing that "whether we live or whether we die, we are the Lord's" (Romans 14:8). Such a faith means that the loved one who dies is not lost because through that one Lord, the Lord both of the living and the dead, there is a form of communion with those who have gone before.

About these things, most Christians of every denomination will agree. Where the variations in belief come is when different denominations get more specific not about what God does but about how God does it. However, differences on the *how* should not obscure the fact that Christian churches have in common the belief that life and death are in the hands of a gracious God. The hope, the victory and the promise are shared by all.

Not everyone, of course, is religiously inclined. Atheists flatly deny that a God exists. For them, reliance on the supernatural or supranatural is unwarranted at best, misguided superstition in any event and harmful to self and others at worst. Death is a simple and absolute end to existence.

While agnostics do not share the atheist's certainty that there is no God, neither does the agnostic share the believer's faith that there is. Agnostics are not willing to take what the Danish theologian Soren Kierkegaard called "the leap of faith." The agnostic answer to the spiritual questions a death raises would be, "There is no way to know — and I cannot rely on what I do not know."

Depending upon your orientation, you may be disappointed in this treatment of alternative spiritual beliefs. We either have said far too much about the spiritual for your tastes, or far too little about something that you feel is at the center of your life. There is no single answer that seems to satisfy everyone — and yet death presents a situation where we really, desperately want answers!

D Rosalene liked to send me messages by clipping out newspaper articles that spoke to us on a current problem. One of her last clippings to me was a cartoon showing a person looking up at the stars on a clear night. The caption read, "The task is to learn to live without the answers."

Whatever your faith or spiritual belief, it is certain that it will be tested during your grief work, as will be your intellectual and emotional resources. For some, the testing will end and a new, more solid, comforting faith will result. For others, the death of your spouse will raise spiritual questions that you may wrestle with for the rest of your life. The very basic foundations of your lifestyle may be shaken. The paradox of life for survivors is that with the joy of love, we must suffer the despair of grief. While some deny or are doubtful about any larger meaning of life, a faith helps us to see grief through. The time will come for each of us to find out what is on the other side of death. Until that time comes, the question remains, "How, then, shall we live?" Our spiritual beliefs are integral to the way we answer that question.

We have now presented the basic framework of our model of grief. To the five tasks — to acknowledge, feel, substitute, detach and reconstruct — we bring four kinds of resources — the physical, intellectual, emotional and spiritual. The interaction of these tasks and resources (5 x 4) results in the 20 Steps of Grief.

There is, however, one further factor we want to keep in mind as you go through the model. We believe that how you experience your grief and how you respond through the 20 Steps of Grief will be affected by your personality. In Chapter 7 we'll say more about how your personality is related to grief, but so you can keep these thoughts in mind as you work through our model, we'll give you a brief introduction now.

Personality And Grief

Personality is a term that comprises the habitual patterns or qualities of behavior that characterize you as a unique person. Our experience indicates that most people in grief are not able to make conscious use of their personality strengths so long as they are in shock or are overwhelmed by their feelings. After healing begins, personality factors can be integrated more helpfully in the process.

One of the most helpful theories of personality comes from the Swiss psychiatrist Carl G. Jung. Jung believed that much of human behavior can be explained by using his way of looking at personality. He identified eight primary psychological types. Jung observed that people orient themselves to the world differently according to whether they are "extraverted" or "introverted." He also said that people have different ways of taking in information and different ways of making decisions about the information they take in. In summary, Jung said:

1. We have an innate predisposition to *extraversion* or to *introversion,* depending on whether we are energized by people, events, things, etc., in the outer world, or energized by the inner world of ideas, concepts and impressions, etc.
2. We take in information about the world around us through either *sensing* perception or *intuitive* perception.
3. We make judgments about what we perceive either by analytical *thinking* or by rationally applying a hierarchy of personal and person-centered *feeling* values.

The Myers-Briggs Type Indicator

Katherine Briggs and her daughter, Isabel Myers, based their development of the Myers-Briggs Type Indicator® (MBTI™) on Jung's theory. The MBTI is a personality preference *indicator,* not a test. Briggs and Myers were able to expand Jung's eight personality types to 16 by identifying whether persons prefer to use their perception or their judgment in the outer world, which makes it possible then to determine what an individual's *dominant* or preferred personality gift is.

Extraverts express their dominant gift primarily in the outer world while introverts prefer to use their dominant gift primarily in the inner world. We believe that a person's dominant personality gift is very much involved in how that person manages and recovers from grief.

The 16 possible personality types come from the various combinations of the four basic preferences. According to the theory, we may prefer:

1. Either Extraversion or Introversion (i.e., E or I)
2. Either Sensing or Intuitive perception (i.e., S or N)
3. Either Thinking or Feeling judgment (i.e., T or F)
4. Either a Judging (which does not mean judgmental) or a Perceptive attitude to the world (i.e., J or P)

Obviously 16 personality types cannot explain all the infinite variety that exists in human behavior. Because we are each a unique creation with a different life history, there are significant differences among people who exhibit even the same personality types in this model. But it can help to explain human behavior if we have a systematic way of looking at it even though Jung's theory may be only one representation of reality. It gives us an important and useful method of communicating with each other about behavior when some common frame of reference is available. People in grief desperately need a common form of communication between survivors and care-givers. When interpreted by a qualified professional, the Myers-Briggs Type Indicator (MBTI) provides such a common language.

The MBTI is a scientifically validated psychological instrument that can help determine what personality type you prefer. If you can find a qualified professional to administer and interpret this instrument, it may help greatly toward your healing. (Guidance in finding such a qualified person is given in Gary's *Afterword*.)

The way this MBTI model of personality usually is presented can be seen in Table 1.2.

In Chapter 7 we'll explain all four of these MBTI scales, but for now the most important for our purposes are the middle two scales: Sensing or Intuitive types of perception and Thinking or Feeling types of rational judgment.

The key to applying the MBTI model of personality functions to the 20-step model of grief work lies in relating the functions to the energy resources. It may be assumed that a person who prefers as the dominant mode the use of Sensing perception will naturally emphasize the physical aspects in grief. The dominant Sensing person

Table 1.2 — MBTI Model Of Personality

(E) Extraversion _____ | _____ Introversion (I)
                  Outer or Inner World/Source of Energy

(S) Sensing _____ | _____ Intuition (N)
            Perception: Way of Taking in Information

(T) Thinking _____ | _____ Feeling (F)
              Judgment: Decision-Making

(J) Judgment _____ | _____ Perception (P)
              What Outside World Sees: Lifestyle

could, however, have a harder time making use of the more intuitive spiritual resources. The dominant Intuitive person may emphasize spiritual energy in response to grief but may overlook or neglect basic physical and material needs. The person who prefers Thinking judgment may emphasize intellectual energy but may tend to keep looking for intellectual answers while burying feelings or being out of touch with them. The dominant Feeling type person may be more at home with emotions but could be stressed when forced to use the thinking function to analyze the situation and make an objective decision about what next steps to take.

Most people seem to exhibit strengths in some functions and weaknesses in others. The way you put these personality preferences to work in your relations with other people makes up the unique person that you are. And they also will affect the way you go through grief.

So far as we know, no one has approached grief in the comprehensive way we do in this book, integrating grief theories, personality theory and a whole-person perspective. We hope our work will be helpful to you as you take the steps of grief that lead to reconstruction and that it will find its way into a new, more effective form of counseling the bereaved.

Before you turn to the first task of grief, to Acknowledge, we have a final word we think may be useful to you. M. Scott Peck suggests that life is a continual process of meeting and solving problems. Life requires energy and is painful. There can be no life without both joy and suffering. When we can accept the suffering, we are free to experience the joy more fully. But to live life successfully requires discipline and Peck suggests that discipline involves deferral of gratification, responsibility, honesty and balance.

Deferring Gratification

Delaying gratification is a process of scheduling the pain and pleasure of life. By experiencing the present pain you are making an investment in your future wholeness.

Responsibility

Responsibility requires that we accept our problems as our own rather than try to avoid the necessity of solving them or hoping that others will take care of our needs. In grief, you must take responsibility for the rest of your life. To confront the fact that there is no one who can really take on our grief for us can be infuriating. Your relationship with D _____ may have conditioned you into being dependent and maybe even helpless on your own. Nevertheless, it is now up to you to go on without D _____. You will have to draw on the physical, intellectual, emotional and spiritual resources that you may have permitted to atrophy for a long time. They are still there. They just need to be dusted off and exercised again. Like any muscle that hasn't been used for a while, it will hurt at first to put them back to work. A Chinese proverb in a fortune cookie said, "There is nothing in life except what you put there." You helped to create your past and now you must think about creating your future. More than think about it, you need to do it — and, with appropriate help, we are confident you can!

Honesty

Honesty requires that we become dedicated to exploring the mysteries of life, ever redefining our understanding of the world as it constantly changes. In grief, you must re-evaluate your previously developed lifestyle and re-establish your self-image before you can go on to be the different person you are becoming.

Balance

Balancing requires that we learn flexibility and that we apply the other three traits in our relationships with others in healthy ways. A balance is needed in the work of grief because all four requirements of physical, intellectual, emotional and spiritual needs must be met for healthy recovery and reconstruction to emerge. The description of grief work that follows applies that balance to each of the tasks we experience in the process of loss and recovery.

It is time now to take a break, review this material if you wish and then plan to get on with the work. Please understand that the order of presentation is merely a convenience since some sequence must be observed in a book. You can refer back to the diagram of 20 steps of grief (in Table 1.1) to locate where you are, according to the numbered sections throughout the book. After you read it through sequentially once, then you may find it useful to go back to the individual numbered sections that spoke most meaningfully to you.

2

Acknowledge

Every minute about four people die in the United States, 24 hours a day, seven days a week. Until it happens to somebody in your family, you may not care. Now it has happened to your spouse and you do care, infinitely. It has also happened to you and all the close members of your family, co-workers, friends and others who came into contact with your spouse on a regular basis. None of you wanted it to happen, but it did. Now D _____ is dead and gone. You hate it, but there it is. The loss upsets your life in every way. You wonder if you can go on living without D _____. It lies over your head like a black, menacing thundercloud on one of those hot, stifling summer days just before a storm breaks over the horizon. Your head buzzes, your heart palpitates, you sweat and you may feel panic. You can scarcely put one foot in front of the other. You want to roll back the calendar to happier times, you want the world to stop and pay its respects, you want people to hurt with you and you may want revenge for this unspeakable assault on your life.

The burden is unbearable, yet you bear it. You may feel like a fish on a hook; if you fight it, you do more damage to yourself and if you don't fight it, you will lose altogether. You are caught in a paradox; you can't live without D _____ and yet you are doing just that. Your mind is a jumble of confused, random thoughts that don't add up to anything.

If you did not breathe involuntarily, you might stop completely. It doesn't matter how many years you had together; they were not enough. You know it happened because your memory tells you so, but you wish it hadn't. You don't want to believe that it did, but you know you have no choice. Now you will need to apply all your coping resources for crisis management to your changed life circumstances. It will not be easy or quick.

John Bowlby discovered that the first reaction to horrifying loss is an indignant protest. Your life has been assaulted and you demand redress but unlike rape or physical assault or divorce, there may be no one you can blame as the culprit. So you are frustrated in your attempt at protest and you may sink into despair. You may frantically try to avoid the feeling of hopelessness that engulfs you by attempting to run away from it. One widow rolled up 30,000 miles on her new car in less than a year, just trying to run away from acknowledging the death of her husband. You may deny the loss and attempt to avoid its ghastly implications to your lifestyle by not giving yourself permission to face up to it. If you don't acknowledge the loss, you may get stuck in this first reaction and remain in protest or denial for a long time. Adapting to your new life will be delayed and possibly even aborted if you cannot work through your first reaction to the death of your spouse. As soon as possible, you should begin work on this first task of acknowledgment. It will probably leave a bad taste in your mouth and you may wish you could do anything but swallow it, but only by taking it in, digesting it and letting it go will you be free.

Physical Acknowledgment (Step 1)

The physical response to death is prompted by your sensory perception. You need to see it, touch it, hear it, smell it and measure it through a stilled heartbeat, a lack of blood pressure, a cold body.

Physically, I remembered the times we had together when she was well, healthy and active in my life. I remembered what it felt like to hold her, to make love with her, to wake up with her, to vacation with her, to eat with her, to keep house with her, to argue with her, to raise a family with her, to live with her, to grow with her. I also remembered how she died. The effect of the cause of death on her body. How she looked during those last few weeks. How she looked at the end. How she looked at me at the end. How she died at the end. It replayed in my mind over and over, like a continuous video tape in full color.

The replay is a necessary part of healing, painful as it may be. Each time you suffer through the replay, it gets a tiny bit easier. One day you will notice that the pain actually is lessening. Someday it will be tolerable.

And you remember the funeral arrangements. The selection of a casket, arrangements for the service, the flowers, the setting, the body. Ah, the body. There actually are several bodies in your memory. The beautiful one you married, the live one when D _____ was well, the sick one or the one at death, the one just shortly after death, and the one they displayed in the casket at the funeral.

There are those who think that viewing the body really helps to internalize the fact that a death has occurred. You need to ask yourself whether or not you had enough goodbye time with the physical body to fully absorb the impact of death. In times past, family members actually helped prepare the body for burial or disposal. When the embalmer came to the house, the family helped him prepare the body for viewing in the living room. Things are done differently today. Not being involved with preparing the body may shield us from the full impact of dealing with the death on a physical plane. But deal with it we must. So we deal with it gradually over a longer period of time, through memory.

Then there are the physical things at home. All the personal possessions, the photographs, the household items your spouse used and touched. I had to deal with her personal effects in the closets, the kitchen, the bathroom and the bedroom. Her favorite chairs in the living room and at the dining table. Her reading and project materials. Her side of the bed. When I lifted the sheets on our bed for the first time after my D Rosalene died, there was her night-gown that she wore only a few days before. I could scarcely touch

it. So I slept on the couch in the living room for several weeks. And
you can imagine how I felt about her clothing, makeup, jewelry
and other personal items.

It may take some time before you are ready to deal with all these
physical possessions of your spouse. Take your time. Recycle the
memories of those last events frequently and often. That is the way
your mind heals itself and learns to accommodate the trauma you
have experienced. Remove personal items only as you can muster
the strength. That is a part of detachment that can only come later,
after you have worked on acknowledgment for a while.

Slowly, ever so slowly, you can reclaim the physical space as your
own so far as it makes you feel better to do so. This may include
selling or giving away *D's* _____ personal possessions or redecorating the space, including painting and new furnishings. You may even want to relocate. This should be done very
carefully and only after enough time has passed to assure clear
thinking. Don't let any others set your timetable for you. We will be
saying that over and over again. For now, just remember and weep.
Eventually you will begin to believe the unbelievable.

Your physical reaction to grief may include sensations of distress
that occur in waves which seem to threaten your own life. These
symptoms can include a tightness in the throat, a choking sensation
with difficulty in swallowing, shortness of breath, muscle weakness,
the need for sighing, spontaneous crying, nausea or a feeling of
emptiness in the abdomen, loss of taste, sleeplessness and sweating.
These physical symptoms can be so fearsome that you may try to
avoid any activity that seems to enhance them. You may resist speaking of the deceased person or refuse visits by friends or relatives that
bring back the unpleasant memories or deliberately avoid thoughts
of *D* _____ or even mentioning the name.

Such reactions are all understandable as you try to avoid the
horrifying mental pain, but confronting the loss in all its grisly
terror is the only way to overcome your fear of the future. Bottling
up the reactions to grief has been known to cause disease and even
death among survivors. Horrifying as the reactions may seem, the
most healthy response is to permit yourself to experience them
fully. As you learn to live with these physical reactions, they will
become less and less disabling. You will gradually gain more and
more confidence in your ability to control and eventually conquer
them. If you continue to suppress these reactions, they may erupt

at some future time when a seemingly unrelated crisis can open all
these incompletely healed wounds.

Intellectual Acknowledgment (Step 2)

The intellectual acknowledgment of death demands order and
logic. The thinking survivor needs a reasonable explanation for the
unanswerable questions — Why? Why now? Why that way? Why
D _____? Why not me? Logic fails. Yet the intellectual need for answers remains. It is another paradox of grief.

Your mind may have difficulty accepting the fact that your
D _____ died. However the death occurred,
whether by natural causes, accident, suicide or homicide, the result
is the same. D _____ is gone and is not com-
ing back. You can say that but it is difficult to believe. Denial is an
acceptable defense mechanism for a time but eventually it must
be overcome by reality. You can begin the intellectual task with a
simple syllogism:

All people die.
D _____ was a person.
Therefore, eventually, D _____ would have to die.
Or
Medicine can prolong life but not sustain it.
Medicine did all that it could.
Therefore, medicine could not sustain the life of
D _____.

*Maybe you still can't believe it for a while. Even D Rosalene could
not believe it when the nurse said, "There is no more pulse." D
Rosalene opened her eyes, looked up at the clock on the wall and
locked her gaze onto mine as if to say, "I don't believe this is
happening to me." It happened to us. My memory tells me so. It was
incredible. I still don't want to believe it.*

At this stage you are not asked to accept it, only to acknowledge
it. When Mother Teresa was asked how she could keep on going in
her futile battle against mass starvation in India, she is said to have
replied, "We are not called to be successful but to be faithful." You
are now called to believe even though your mind rebels at its belief.
You may not be completely successful in your acceptance of the
death of your spouse but you must remain faithful in your attempt
to acknowledge it. Your sanity and your mental health demand it.

How can one pursue logic in the face of the illogical? There just is no appropriate intellectual answer to the *Why* that screams within us. The mind concludes that when the heart stops, the body dies. The mind knows there was a time when D _____ did not physically exist, then a time that D _____ did exist and now a time that D _____ does not exist again. But what is time? What is existence? What is life, what is death, what is sleep, what is . . . ? How does one live without the answers?

How can the finite mind know the Infinite? How many times can one walk half the distance from here to a wall? No matter how many times we do it, there still remains an infinite number of attempts to go. The intellect has real limitations and nowhere is this more apparent than in the face of death. Some things may be impossible for us to understand and some things really are unknowable. Yet we continue the intellectual search. That is the way we are made.

Trying to resolve an unresolvable loss intellectually can trigger obsessional thinking about it.

When I awoke in the morning, thoughts about all my losses were overwhelming for a long time. Rosalene (my wife) is gone. Emmert (my father-in-law) is gone. Thelma (my mother-in-law) is gone. Ruth (my stepmother-in-law) is gone. My father and mother are both gone. Both my children have moved away from home. I am alone.

Trying to suppress such thoughts to avoid the pain of acknowledgment only reinforces it until it saturates your consciousness. The vivid memories connected to significant losses contribute to symptoms of post-trauma shock not unlike that of a combat veteran. Friends and relatives may try to distract you with invitations to a variety of activities to take your mind off the shock or you may force yourself to think about something else. According to Daniel Wegner, such self-distractions are useful only for a short time because the obsessional thoughts soon return to consciousness, demanding some resolution. He suggests that the best way to deal with painful, obsessional thoughts is to stop trying to stop them and permit yourself to go ahead and think the unthinkable. Facing up to unwanted thoughts is to fight your enemy because self-distraction is little more than running away. It is only a quick fix.

Consciously replacing mental control with the acknowledgment that we are powerless over life and death is the first step toward regaining peace of mind. It may be the only way to peace. As much as you can, try to face your painful thoughts and memories. Deal with them openly and eventually they will begin to dissipate. It is important to apply your attention to your grief and find a solution in order to manage all the problems your loss represents. Thinking the unwanted thoughts over and over can only lead to more distress if the underlying feelings are not worked through. If you are prone to depression, it may be more difficult for you to stop recycling negative, unwanted thoughts. *If your thoughts become dangerous to you, it is definitely time to seek professional help.* Sometimes another perspective from a professional can help break the cycle.

Our intellectual dilemma might be described in this verse by an anonymous author, shared by a beloved friend:

> My life is but a weaving, between my God and me.
> I do not choose the colors, He works so steadily.
> Ofttimes He weaves in sorrow and I, in foolish pride,
> Forget He sees the upper, and I the underside.
> Not 'til the loom is silent and the shuttles cease to fly,
> Will God unroll the canvas, and explain the reasons why.

Emotional Acknowledgment (Step 3)

The death of D _____ demands acknowledgment at the emotional level. You may hate the fact that one you loved has died. And you may feel uncontrolled rushes or tidal waves of many different emotions: fear, anger, anxiety, panic, guilt, jealousy, etc. These will be discussed in the next chapter. For now, be aware that what may best help you to reach acknowledgment is the feeling of love.

Love comes to us in several different forms. There is the love of family members, the love of brotherhood, the erotic or romantic love of a newly paired couple and the unconditional, nonjudgmental love that many associate with God or a Higher Power.

Your relationship with D _____ may have begun with romantic love based on attraction. Peck has explained this attraction as falling in love. He and others also call it "cathexis." This form of pair bonding is being "cathected;" i.e., you cathect the object of your attraction.

We seem to be able to decathect as easily as we cathect. It is a temporary, intense form of attachment that cannot be sustained at that level of and by itself. This pair bonding can occur between a wide variety of different individuals, some desirable and some undesirable. It is not genuine love. Genuine love was called "agape" in the ancient Greek. It describes the complete, unconditional, nonjudgmental love that wants only the physical, intellectual, emotional and spiritual growth of the love object. Genuine love begins to grow only after cathexis fades. "Falling in love" may have declined a few months after the erotic, romantic urge to mate with D _____ subsided. Then you began the building of genuine love. It may have contained an element of the romantic love through all the years but it became something infinitely more.

That genuine love developed from an act of pure will between you two. It was fed by conscious commitment, discipline and mutual attention to the physical, intellectual, emotional and spiritual needs of each other. It sometimes involved confrontation. It sustained each of you as separate but interdependent individuals. It also involved risk.

When you married, it was "till death do us part." Now death has parted you. You are separated in love. The love that cemented you two through the years does not just go away. It is there in a new way. For some, that love continues to sustain them for the rest of their lives. For others, the old love remains but life brings new loves to set beside the old. Before you can be ready for the new, what has changed in your life must be acknowledged emotionally, with love.

Spirituality And Acknowledgment (Step 4)

Acknowledging the death of D _____ spiritually requires that you confront your own spirituality. Depending upon where you are in your own spiritual awareness and development, this confrontation can be either comforting or traumatic. According to Patrick and Thomas Malone, intimacy provides a connectedness with another and a channel to our own souls. In a relationship of true intimacy we are able to be in tune with our spiritual selves, and a sense of wholeness and completeness results. This sense can be experienced in relationships with pets, plants and even stars, but it is achieved best in relationship with another human being. You probably had such intimacy with your spouse. With this person's death, you have lost one channel to your own soul and the awareness of this loss can be among the more devastating of the grief symptoms. Confronting this loss of a portion of your self may be one of the factors in the depression that often follows a loss.

The ego, or self, would have ultimate control of life and seeks to maintain its own position at the center of all our existence. With the event of death even the ego must confront its lack of control, and that can be terrifying. At death, we confront the ultimate contest of control — and we lose. Just as D _____ ultimately had to lay aside a physical body, now we must lay aside the ego drive to control. We must acknowledge that in death, as in much of life, we are really powerless and that we are unable to manage the outcome by sheer force of will. You must turn over control to a Higher Power, God as you understand God, and trust that your will and your life are being conducted by the One whose only purpose is your ultimate good.

Robert and Carol Ann Faucett quoted Carl G. Jung, in his later years, as saying: "I do not believe there is a God, I *know* (there is)." In his experience, this knowledge came from an awareness of what lies deep in the unconscious mind of all humans. Jung called it the "collective unconscious," i.e., the repository of the experiences of the ages.

In the earliest years of our life, we are driven by our physical senses. Our earliest goals are based purely on survival needs. Later we seek fulfillment of our procreation instincts. As we enter mid-life, we become more aware of our intellectual and emotional energy. From mid-life into our later years, Jung believed we have a calling to search out our spiritual nature, possibly in preparation for our ultimate return to the source of our creation.

In our search we may seek spiritual growth through action in physical service to others, personal relationships and the healing of others, isolated contemplation of the subconscious spirit within or analytical review of the logic and order in the universe. We wrestle with the ancient paradox voiced by the Psalmist, "What are we that You are mindful of us? Yet You have created us only a little lower than the angels" (paraphrase of Psalm 8).

So long as we are bound to the physical body, we cannot completely know the truth of the spirit. Nor can we experience the complete joy and peace that is expected by many as they anticipate being with their God. To spiritually acknowledge the death of your D _____ is to believe that life is more than physical, emotional and intellectual. It is to acknowledge that, in some way we now know only in part, the temporal is linked with the eternal.

Since physical life is a journey between the mysteries of birth and death, now the death of D _____ has been a reminder that sometime you, too, will complete that part of the journey but first you must walk the path that is now before you. Whether or not you share the questions of Job, perhaps you can share the Psalmist's spirit: "This is the day that the Lord has made.

Let us rejoice and be glad in it" (Psalm 118:24). Beginning each day with this affirmation can help sustain you while the ultimate spiritual question is being worked out.

3

Feel

You are now a different person. You are no longer a spouse, you are an ex-spouse. *D* _____ has died and you must go on alone. This is hard to do, whether you are female or male. If you are male, particularly a traditional male in our culture, you probably were oriented to keeping your feelings to yourself and suppressing all but the strongest of emotional reactions. You were expected to be strong and in control of all of life's events and most of the time you probably carried out that role successfully. But now, in spite of your heroic attempts at control, you may find yourself experiencing a host of new feelings, some more intense than you ever thought possible. Feelings more devastating than you can explain to friends or family may overwhelm you, as you realize that you are alone. Longing, sadness and loneliness may be your constant companions. You may feel like searching over the whole world to find your lost love. Every person you see is instantly compared to your spouse and you wonder if you will ever again enjoy the intimacy you enjoyed with D _____. The possibility that you might not consumes you in despair and self-pity. The sadness threatens to eat out your bones and as it becomes a part of you, you begin to wonder if even your spouse's return would be sufficient to make you whole again. Your appearance, demeanor, personality, behavior and general presence can be so troubling to people who knew you before that they don't know how to respond.

If your symptoms of grief sound somewhat like the withdrawal symptoms of a drug addict forced to give up his need for a "fix," you are not far from the truth. Modern understanding of emotional addiction and co-dependence point to the possibility that we can be addicted to another person. We can be addicted to the feelings of contentment, safety, security and love that we become accustomed to while living with our lost spouse. Now you must experience all the symptoms of involuntary withdrawal from your attachment to D _____.

It took me four years, many months of expensive psychotherapy and reading through dozens of books to realize how post-World War II social addictions may have contributed to the devastation I suffered at the loss of D Rosalene. Due to the dysfunctional family I experienced, I forfeited a normal teenage life while caretaking for a chronically ill mother and mostly absentee father. The circumstances of my youth predisposed me to see the outer world as dangerous, predatory, a fearful place. I did not develop the resources to defend myself alone. My training for airborne combat in the Air Force reinforced and confirmed that outlook. Through my early marriage at age 21 to a preacher's daughter with a degree in home economics, the subsequent creation of the "perfect family" and an adequate civilian career to maintain them, I built up a fortress of defense against the perceived threat of the outside world of competition and struggle. It served me well for over 30 years. During that time, I shunned the world except when I was at work and possibly stunted my own emotional development. By dealing primarily with ourselves and our family, D Rosalene and I avoided the tensions that would arise from exposure to the wider social environment.

With her death and the simultaneous independence of my children, my fortress was demolished. I was left exposed without my usual defenses. In the empty nest my reaction was panic and confusion. My security blanket was gone! I had to face the world alone.

The only thread of continuity was my work and that also was threatened by executive turnover. Panic was the response. It is traumatic for an addicted lover to re-enter the world after having lost touch with it. It was like being caught in some form of time warp. The abrupt demolition of my fortress left me in disoriented agony.

Since I did not know specifically what I was afraid of, I could not do anything to allay my panic. The anxiety of my parents had at last been transferred to me. Perhaps the realization that many post-World War II adult children carry such an emotional burden can help us all toward the path of healing and self-realization.

When you do not appear to be back to "normal" in a few weeks or months, many of your coupled friends drift away, seeking to avoid the pain of their own future confrontation with death and grief. If you represent what they have to look forward to, they want to avoid it as long as they can. You can't really blame them because that is the way you acted before. In turn, their defection can make you feel more unloved, forsaken, abandoned and alone just when you desperately need to feel loved, supported and protected. You are pressured to behave "normally" by people who do not understand that "abnormal" is normal in your circumstances.

John Bowlby learned, from research with children confined to hospitals, that *the first reaction to forced separation from loved ones may be protest at the outrage that is now forced upon you.* With it may also come a feeling of panic at the sense of abandonment. This in turn can trigger all the feelings of insecurity that are dredged up from all the previous losses we have suffered throughout life that may not have been adequately grieved. We feel out of control and totally alone in our suffering. No one can help carry the burden for us, it seems so *we are likely to revert to childhood behavior,* or even infantile behavior, as we absorb the shock and fear from the loss that is forced upon us. We are thrust back to our birth event, when panic and acute anxiety accompanied our forced separation from the womb. We are now forced to live without the comforting, secure connection through the umbilical to our "mother", i.e., our lost spouse. It is no wonder that friends and relatives who have not experienced such grief cannot relate to us now. Sometimes they only make matters worse as they attempt to force us back into the mainstream of social life before we are able to play the role they want from us. Since we need the support of people so desperately at this time, we may put on a mask of normality when we are around them, only to collapse into despair when we are alone.

Allow Yourself To Feel Intensely

The most important aspect of your feelings of grief is to give yourself permission to experience them in all their intensity. Although their fearsome nature may be horrifying, these are all normal reactions to loss and should be experienced in order to get them out of your system. Of course, saying these feelings are normal is like saying it is normal to experience pain from a broken leg. That may not be very comforting if you have a broken leg. The feelings that accompany acute grief are just as normal, although they may be a new experience and therefore, sensed as life-threatening. But feelings need to be attended to. If you repress them, healing can be slowed down or stifled, making it more difficult and taking longer for you to get over the death of D _____. Alla Bozarth-Campbell has likened our need to permit our feelings a full range of expression to allowing a deep physical wound to heal slowly from the inside out. It must be kept open on the outside to let the draining take place. Sometimes, if it closes over too soon, it may even need to be re-opened by a surgeon (in the case of grief, more likely a professional counselor). This prevents a surface sealing from taking place too quickly, forcing the festering underneath to burrow even deeper and cause more damage. *You need to let the feelings surge through you, flow through you, expressing them with friends or support groups whenever possible,* and flush out your being in all four of the energy quadrants in order to fully recover.

Unfortunately, the "normal" world around you may not tolerate your visible anguish very well. You may need to mask it when you are in the company of those who cannot accept your need for expression. You will need to find the time and place to experience your feelings and express them openly to some caring, nonjudg-mental witness. It is in this expression that healing takes place.

Find Help And Support

Your grief symptoms may be so severe and depleting that you feel the need of professional support, if caring family and friends are not available. We will continue to emphasize that support for the be-reaved is provided by a variety of helpers. Some are professional social workers or clinical psychologists. Pastors and other religious professionals are often trained in caring for the emotional and spir-itual needs of the grief-stricken. Volunteer-led support groups also can be of help. Your church, local mental health agency or family physician should be able to put you in touch with such help. In normal grief all these helpers provide the same function, that of bearing witness to your pain and assuring you that others experience similar dysfunction in grief and eventually recover.

If your grief is causing you to be unable to function, or if others around you express their concern for your well-being, a professional needs to be consulted immediately. You might look for a clinical psychologist or a psychiatrist who specializes in loss. A professional can help determine if psychotherapy, medication or hospital treatment are advisable. More intensive treatment for grief is called for when our crisis management and coping mechanisms are stressed beyond their limits. Even with this kind of professional help, however, you will need to endure for a time until you actually outlive the impact of your feelings. It can seem like the time required is longer than your level of tolerance but part of the key to recovery is knowing that it may take longer than you expected. The feelings of grief can persist for a year or more and sometimes it takes far longer.

Physical Feeling (Step 5)

Practically any physical symptom occurring at this time can be caused by your grief. When the mind is occupied with grief, it cannot manage as well the defense mechanisms usually available to protect your body against disease. The immune system becomes lethargic, letting invaders of all types attack your physical body. Physical responses to grief can be scary. They include heart palpitations, sweating, shaking, headaches, dizziness, disruptions of normal sleep patterns, changes in appetite, weight loss or gain and even symptoms of the same physical illness that *D* _____ suffered. The intensity of these physical symptoms varies from mild to severe.

When I visited our family mountain campsite eight months after *D Rosalene* *died, my heart raced up to 130 beats per minute as I just stood there remembering the happy times she created for us on that spot. It was terrifying.*

Your senses may tell you that something is drastically wrong, adding fear to the physical symptoms. You may fear for your own survival but paradoxically you may think it would just be easier to go to bed some night and not wake up. You may actually contemplate suicide, especially if the symptoms drag on. While not unusual, *any thought of ending it all needs to be discussed immediately with a professional.* Your medical doctor is a good place to begin.

At a minimum you should have a complete physical examination to assure yourself that the physical symptoms are the result of grief and not some actual disease.

You may find it difficult to get adequate sleep. You may awaken often or experience troubling dreams, which are thought by some to be evidence of the subconscious mind trying to work its way out of the maze. If simple remedies like a warm shower and glass of milk before bed do not work, talk these things over with your physician. If you do not find your physician as sensitive or helpful as you need, you can always seek a second opinion from another doctor.

Even though you may not feel like eating, try to maintain a balanced diet and consume a normal amount of calories. Some people report the inability to swallow as food seems to stick in their throat. Five or six small snacks each day may be easier to eat than three large meals. Consider using a microwave oven to warm-up packaged meals quickly without the need for decisions about content and lengthy preparations.

Try to get in some exercise every day. Blair Justice reported research showing that exercise seems to affect the chemistry in the brain in a way that helps to alleviate stress and prevent clinical depression.

I bought a rowing machine and worked out on it at least 30 minutes four or five times per week. During the third year when I began to feel stronger, I joined an exercise club.

Some therapists suggest walking a mile each day. If you cannot do such rigorous exercise, ask your physician what you can do that might help. *Of course, when starting any kind of physical activity, it is important to first check your idea out with your physician.*

As with all the feeling responses to grief, your physical symptoms should subside gradually with enough time but it may take longer than you expected. Be patient with yourself.

Intellectual Feeling (Step 6)

If feelings of grief persist past the time when you expected to be better, your logic may begin to tell you that something more serious is wrong. *This mental attitude can add confusion to your other feelings,* leaving you vulnerable to a variety of faulty behaviors. We know that the mind affects the body in both conscious and unconscious ways. When the mind is damaged, its control functions are disrupted and distorted. Do not condemn yourself for doing things that might have seemed "dumb" to you in normal times past. Take it easy on yourself. You have suffered a severe, numbing shock to your mind. The reaction may be similar to the results of a physical blow to your head, or to the shock of the combat veteran.

Your mental condition may include a kind of befuddlement. You may wander around in a sort of dazed condition. You may begin familiar mental tasks and find yourself unable to complete them.

Even after 36 months I did not feel like balancing my checkbook. For the first time in my life, I wanted help in filling out my tax forms. Knowing I had graduated from college first in my class and I now couldn't do something as simple as balancing my checkbook, I wondered about my overall mental condition.

Until this time of befuddlement clears up, **you should avoid making any long-range decisions that will affect you or your family members in important ways.** This is not the time to relocate, modify your investments or insurance, change jobs, commit to a remarriage or otherwise stress your already overloaded mental capacity.

Your mental attitude may include a lack of motivation. You may not feel like performing even routine chores. Housekeeping, cooking, laundry, lawn mowing, even personal hygiene may be too much bother and not worth the effort. If you work, you may find it extremely difficult to concentrate for more than a few minutes. Your mind may dwell on D _____ and the events surrounding the terminal phase of your loved one's life.

Unfortunately, your productivity may suffer, threatening your job security. This piles anxiety on top of fear. You may need understanding and sympathy from your supervisor and co-workers for much longer than they expect. Even if you are able to hide your symptoms, it is best to be honest with your boss about your inability to be fully productive. Perhaps you could volunteer to work extra hours, if possible, to make up for your slower pace. Give your employer periodic progress reports on your personal life so confidence in your ability to manage your grief will be sustained. If you can take a leave of absence or extended vacation, several weeks away from the job may help to protect your professional image while you deal with your situation.

In public you will be expected to wear a mask of mental normality. Since untrained people may not be able to deal with your suffering, they want you to act normally. It will make them feel better and less uncomfortable around you if you can give them what they want. However, the necessity of giving them what they want will demand great energy and acting ability. You will need to exhibit mental normality by a sheer act of will until your pretended normal state actually becomes normal again in a new form that is appropriate for you.

When the mind cannot cope with personal crises, it sometimes seals off the event to escape the pain. This reaction can lead to a form of depression. There are intellectual methods, called cognitive therapy, for dealing with this development and they will be discussed in the following section of this chapter. For now, permit yourself to experience the mental anguish that comes with grief and rely on the fact that others have experienced this same state of befuddlement and worked their way through it back to control and a form of mental health. It isn't easy or quick but it is possible, even though you will live without many of the answers you seek about what has happened to you and D _____.

Emotional Feeling (Step 7)

The emotions of grief may shock you with their intensity. If you have not experienced such intense feelings before, their power to disrupt your normal behavior is such that *you may feel intense fear.* Please be assured that these feelings are all manageable. While intensity and duration vary with the situation and they can be disabling for many months, most survivors learn to tolerate their impact and manage through this phase of grief without total dysfunction. Unfortunately, many of your associates, friends and relatives will not understand your emotional plight at this time. Their ignorance can add discomfort to your already fearful state.

Sadness is a normal reaction to the loss of love and companionship that you shared. The feeling of sadness is tender, realistic and desirable. It will enhance your humanity and add depth to the meaning of life, according to David Burns. He says sadness involves a flow of feelings and therefore should have a time limit. However, the sadness that accompanies the loss of D _____ can take several different forms. At times it may drive you inward and sap away all your interest in doing anything. At other times it can stimulate you to feverish activity, such as trying to run away from it all or rushing about searching for your lost spouse in meaningless activities. It may cause you to cry bitterly or it may actually prevent you from crying. If you can cry, there can be a healthy purging of your emotions, so permit yourself to cry, openly if necessary, in public if you feel like it. In short, give yourself permission to mourn for as long as you need.

Through the sadness you may also suffer from deeper feelings of fear, anger, anxiety, guilt, jealousy, panic and depression. These emotions can come at you one at a time, in combination or all together. When they do, it is good to have others you can lean on. But in grief, you may feel completely alone since no one can possibly share your experience of life with the lost loved one. That sense of isolation can breed feelings of abandonment which leave you even more fearful.

Maggie Scarf has explained that when we are in love with someone we resonate with a part of our own inner self that goes back to subconscious memories of our original loved one in infancy, our mother. Some suggest this memory goes back even before birth. What we seek in a mate may be one who can help us to contact archaic yet powerfully meaningful aspects of our inner selves (hence the term "soul mates"). From this perspective, the marriage partner is the person who connects us to parts of our being lost to our conscious memory but still well remembered at almost a cellular level. Falling in love provides a rapturous feeling of engulfment in a safe, intimate world in which perfect nurturance exists, not unlike a return to the womb. It is in marriage that we resurrect the intensity of our first attachment feelings. The breaking of such a union by premature death reawakens old visions of disappointment and alarms, fears of separation, fears of loss, and the worst of all human threats, the infantile nightmare of abandonment. It is no wonder that our emotional reaction to this unspeakable assault on our sense of security and self-esteem is protest, followed often by despair.

Anger may also pain you every waking moment for longer than you expect. Your anger is an appropriate response to being deprived of someone you valued very highly. You may feel outrage at your loss of D _____ and your anticipated life together. Your rage may be directed at the doctors, hospital or emergency staff, yourself, anyone else involved and God. You may even feel hatred toward your lost spouse, the one who died and left you in this miserable condition. Though we realize people do not get sick and die because they want to hurt us, we can still feel wronged by a loved one who died and left us just when we needed them the most. If we are religious the hurt we feel may lead to anger or *hatred toward God, which may cause guilt.*

Guilt is not only a feeling related to religious beliefs. There are ambivalent aspects to every marriage. You can think of things you will not miss about D _____ as well as the many things you will miss. No marriage is a perfect relationship, and none of us is a perfect spouse because we are all human. There may have been times in your marriage when you actually wanted to end it. Or times when you were tempted by some potential replacement who seemed more desirable at the time. You may actually have been unfaithful on some occasions or fantasized about unfaithfulness. Thinking of such times can make you feel guilty. Now it is easy to recall all the times you made D _____ unhappy. *You tend to dwell on all the things you did or did not do that you wish you could do over differently.* Some of this guilt can go back a long way in your marriage and some of it lies closer at hand related to the care your spouse received or did not receive during the last stages.

I felt acute guilt over the fact that I continued to go to work during the last weeks of D Rosalene's hospital care. It was only during the last few days that I stayed with her constantly, and afterward I wondered how I could have been so stupid and insensitive to her condition for the previous two weeks. At the time, I was saving my vacation days to be at home with her when she was released from the hospital.

You may long for another chance and you can beat yourself emotionally, doing penance because you cannot obtain forgiveness from D _____, who is gone. Of course, you can give yourself equal praise for the many more times you made D _____ happy. That ability may come along gradually as you finally move into reconstruction. As you punish yourself, *you may tend to elevate your spouse in memory.* D _____ may become idealized, placed on a pedestal, larger and more perfect in death than in life. You will slowly find it possible to forgive yourself for the many things you need to let go of, and gradually you will be able to think of D _____ more realistically, with all the imperfections and vices included. Even then you may still experience lingering guilt as the tasks of grief tend to overlap. Your guilt will continue to cause you emotional suffering until you decide you have completed penance to make up for all the unhappiness you caused D _____ and have received forgiveness — from God, from D _____ and from yourself. We will discuss the role of forgiveness more in a later section of this book related to reconstruction.

Difficult as guilt is to deal with, *shame may be equally painful.* Psychologists are only now beginning to realize and investigate the immense role of shame in emotional health. If parents do not respond with empathy and attention to children's efforts to perform, they grow up feeling inferior and unlovable. Children's sense of not being affirmed or supported in their strivings leave them feeling that the world does not respond to them at all. For such people in adult grief, just to feel anything other than self-sufficiency — such as a need for support, attention or physical contact — is a source of shame. *If you find it difficult to solve problems you depended on your spouse to take care of, shame can result.* This occurs quite often as close friends and relatives withdraw or play the role of parent in trying to get the grieving person to perform normally in social situations despite their disability. In fact, close relatives and friends may feel shame and withdraw because of your inability to behave normally, which only makes your situation worse. The implicit rule not to talk about painful life experiences only intensifies the shame.

There are two basic antidotes for shame. One is to laugh at yourself, an observation made by Freud. If you can laugh at your own feelings of humiliation, shame will drop immediately but this is very difficult to do in grief. The other resource is to admit feelings of shame openly to a caring witness — a close friend or a therapist — who will respond with nonjudgmental love and respect for your honesty. Your healing may be hastened if you can talk about events and feelings that you may have never disclosed to anyone before.

Envy is another common feeling during this time in your recovery. When you see other healthy couples enjoying life together, you may feel intense jealousy. Why should they be so happy when you are so sad and so deprived of that relationship that you valued so highly? Life just is not fair. No amount of explanation or theories about why some people are subjected to untimely loss can be comforting to you now. You may be jealous of younger couples because they have so much time together ahead of them. And you may be jealous of older couples because they have had so much more time together than you did with D _____.

It is normal to feel jealousy, so don't pile guilt on top of your jealousy. Recognize that your coupled friends may feel guilty around you for their happiness. The result can be alienation of long-standing friendships, as neither you nor they know how to bridge that gap which has now come between you. They may begin to avoid you and you may no longer feel comfortable around them if you both cannot communicate and accept your new feelings about each other.

Such is life. It may be a long time before you are able to accept the happiness of others as a matter of fact.

Anxiety is one of the more troubling feelings for those who have suffered a loss. Anxiety is a most complex emotion. Rollo May and Carol Becker describe it as a terrifying feeling of helplessness after recognizing that danger is looming, without knowing what the exact danger is or how to defend against it. Panic may be a severe form of anticipatory anxiety. It is characterized by a sudden, overwhelming surge of anxiety, experienced both physiologically and subjectively, that reaches a peak in several minutes. It is often accompanied by such physical symptoms as elevated heart rate, palpitations, chest pain, choking, nausea, dizziness, feeling of unreality, burning or prickling of the skin, hot or cold flashes, sweating, faintness, trembling, fear of dying and fear of losing control or going crazy. David Barlow and Jerome Cerny suggest there may be an inherited tendency toward anxiety in some people, making them vulnerable under certain conditions of stress, as some other people may be vulnerable to ulcers.

Anxiety resembles fear, but its effects are less dramatic although sometimes quite severe. Fear usually stimulates an appropriate and immediate fight or flight response, but *anxiety results in a feeling of helplessness.* It may include a feeling of being trapped in a threatening situation from which there is no exit. Sources of anxiety in humans include ancient fears of annihilation, abandonment and loss of love. When we are abandoned by someone we love, this can trigger the entire mechanism of helpless infantile anxiety, bringing desolation and pain compounded by an inexplicable terror such as an infant may experience at the forcible separation from its mother at birth.

Everyone experiences anxiety from time to time but grief can bring it on in such intensity that mental health is threatened. *Anxiety can immobilize you and cause near intellectual and emotional paralysis,* blocking you from keeping up with even the most routine aspects of living and working. You can feel totally helpless in a situation that you cannot alter. You envision loss of your entire normal lifestyle and social moorings since your sense of safety and harmony have been taken away, replaced with a hostile environment and loss of control. *You can become disoriented and uncertain* about your very existence in the world. Caught between a past self that needs to be transformed and a future self that still must be developed, you may become uncertain about how to live in the present. *Anxiety can sap strength from doing even routine tasks in life and work that you have previously mastered, leaving you with fears of losing your mind, your job, your friends.* In turn, such fears can fuel the anxiety, creating a vicious circle of defeat. Anxiety can be either a block to future growth or a catalyst for action. It is a struggle between life and death, growth and stagnation. It leads us to anticipation, our ability to fear and envision what has not yet occurred. Through the death of your spouse comes change, imbalance and the anticipation of danger. Anxiety will always accompany the unknown; it may be unwanted, but it is the unavoidable motivation to change.

Fear, panic, anger, guilt, jealousy and anxiety may lead you into depression. *Anxiety and depression often go together, one masking the symptoms of the other.* Some situational depression goes with the sadness. It may occur shortly after the loss or around three to six months after the death, about the time you expect to start feeling better. It can last several weeks or months. If you experience a tendency toward total withdrawal from life, loss of hope for improvement, with psychic numbness that threatens your will to live, **you may be clinically depressed.** See your physician, a clinical psychologist or a psychiatrist immediately! Medication is available that can help with the kinds of depression that do not respond to psychotherapy alone.

Depression was thought by Freud to be guilt or anger turned inward, directed at oneself as a form of self-hatred or self-blame, or rage at the loss of a source of self-esteem. Verena Kast, a Jungian psychotherapist, has formulated the mourning process into the phases of shock and denial, emotional chaos, searching and separation, and creating a new relationship with oneself and the world. Kast reported research that indicates depression is a likely result of being unable to take leave of lost relationships.

To conquer depression, we must come to terms with our losses. We must learn to relinquish what we have loved and lost in our lives in order to go on with our future. Kast says that people with low self-esteem have more difficulty coping with loss because it reduces their self-worth even further, and they are likely to become chronically depressed. Such people may remain stuck in the past, trying to hang onto the source of their identity in order to avoid the pain of isolation and feeling of abandonment. Until they break loose of the past, develop a new internal source of identity and grow their own supply of self-esteem, depression may be their constant companion.

Another source of depression may be perceived helplessness, believing your actions do not matter, you cannot influence the course of your life, you have come to the end of your coping resources. Biological theories suggest depression arises from changes in the neurotransmission of chemicals which affect the way we think and feel. Many depressed individuals can identify parents or close relatives who were chronically depressed, suggesting a possible inherited component.

Research by Drs. Aaron T. Beck and David D. Burns, psychiatrists at the University of Pennsylvania, has suggested the feelings of anxiety, panic and depression arise primarily from faulty logic in the way we think about negative events that happen to us. They believe sadness is a logical but time-limited reaction to negative events. *The symptoms of chronic depression, however, result more from negative thinking about realistically negative events than the events themselves.* Some people seem to be more likely to look on the positive side of life for some reason, while others seem to become anxious, panicky and depressed through their negative thinking. If you can change your thinking patterns and use more realistic logic this theory says you can alleviate the symptoms of depression.

People who are depressed usually need external help in learning to think positively because their ability to do so has decreased. Research reported by Daniel Wegner indicates that people who are prone to depression are more likely to follow one negative thought automatically with others until a perception of hopelessness is created. They don't seem to be able to counter negative thoughts with positive thoughts because their automatic thinking process keeps pushing more negative thoughts into their consciousness. Merely being around happy people, going to pleasant places and looking at good things are not enough to break the dismal mood of depressed people, as they are for normal people. Unfortunately, normal people often are bewildered by the symptoms of depression in others. *Professional counseling may be needed to provide the kind of help not available from friends or relatives.*

Cognitive Psychotherapy

Beck and Burns have shown that depression can be alleviated effectively and reliably, with and without medication, if patients can be taught to think differently about their circumstances, with a more positive rather than negative orientation. This "cognitive" method depends upon learning how to recognize your faulty thinking and how to apply corrective thinking so your depressing reactions to negative events can be neutralized and even reversed.

Through cognitive psychotherapy, I learned I had been persecuting myself with unreasonable, illogical and negative thoughts. It came as a surprise to me to realize that much of my pain and suffering was being caused by my reaction to her death rather than my actual loss of D Rosalene. I was telling myself that I could not continue to exist and function, much less grow, without her or some substitute in my life. I was asking myself why I should even try. A cognitive therapist helped me to see the ways to overcome such things as all or nothing/black and white reasoning, overgeneralizing, jumping to conclusions, magnification and minimizing, and the "shoulds." My early life training had included concepts of control and responsibility for others that were unrealistic in my new circumstances. Letting go of these "cognitions" was extremely difficult and took a long time.

Cognitive therapy is only one of a number of ways that depression is treated. Dr. Michael Yapko suggests that depression is a very complex disorder, possessing many different dimensions and many different aspects. He grouped causative factors into biological theories, intrapersonal (internal to the individual) theories, and interpersonal (involving other people in the client's social network) theories. An appropriate treatment strategy must be based on a careful diagnosis, since treatment should be individualized depending upon the specific conditions in each case. Your best first step is a consultation with your family physician, who may refer you to a psychologist or a psychiatrist. Don't let pride or an acceptance of cultural standards of stoic self-reliance prevent you from seeking professional help. Those who need professional care and do not get it may despair of life itself. If they become self-destructive, their remaining family will pay a very high emotional price. Some grieving people may resort to addictions such as alcohol or promiscuous sexuality to escape the pain. Such extreme reactions are simply forms of self-destructive behavior. The wiser course, more caring of both yourself and others, is to seek the help you need to get you through this difficult time.

Support Network

If the cost of professional help is a major concern for you, most communities have mental health agencies that will not turn anyone away for lack of funds. While there may also be a trusted friend willing to listen to your feelings and concerns, be aware that you will probably want to repeat and repeat your feelings more often and for longer than your friends or family want to hear about them. Since untrained "volunteers" do not know how to respond, they may become irritated by their own frustration and wander off, leaving you feeling even more alone and abandoned.

Phyllis Silverman concluded from her studies with widows that the best caregiver to a bereaved spouse is one who experienced such a loss earlier and now is strong enough to be a witness to others. She encouraged volunteer networks among the widowed to make such care possible. You may also benefit from becoming part of a support group who can share with its members. *Many local community organizations and churches sponsor widowed groups that are able to help.* Many have found solid support from Parents Without Partners, The Widowed Persons Service (a service of the American Association of Retired People) and They Help Each Other Spiritually (THEOS). Look for a chapter of each in your local area. Sometimes services provided by hospice or funeral directors include followup care for survivors. If you can't locate a support group, perhaps you can start one by inviting other grieving people in your community to meet with you regularly, using this book as a meeting guide.

Here is a personal suggestion to survivors who have been taught to be stoic sufferers. You may have been so successfully taught that your social role in our culture is to be unemotional, rational and intellectual that you have difficulty venting your emotions of grief. You may just try to swallow the feelings of grief and stoically pretend to the world that you can handle it alone. Such behavior can lead to physical illness, despondency and even suicide.

Don't be bashful or embarrassed about letting close friends, co-workers and family know how you really feel. Traditional males in our culture do not build up many male friends in a "buddy" system during marriage, as do many women. Men may need to search out and develop a new group of single people who can be your friends. Your true friends will be understanding and tolerant and you do not need any other kind. Even if you can develop only a few good friends, the benefits will be well worth the effort. More will be said of this in the coming chapter on reconstruction.

Spirituality And Feeling (Step 8)

Even though you may not be a "religious" person, you may find the loss of spiritual intimacy with your spouse to be a major source of pain. Patrick and Thomas Malone called our "intima" the bridge to our souls. It is the innermost part of our being. Intimacy with another provides the sense of being in touch with our real selves. When we are close to another, we know that person in our presence; when we are intimate with another, we know ourselves in their presence. Spiritual intimacy with another person is the way we can experience our real selves most deeply and directly. The loss of that intimacy can be very keenly felt.

In one of the Psalms there is a verse: "My God, my God, why hast thou forsaken me?" (Psalm 22:1). Even persons of great faith at times feel disconnected from their spiritual source. If you are a religious person, try to *keep in mind that it is normal to feel spiritually abandoned when confronted with the death of someone you dearly love.* The intuitive mind searches for a window to the spirit but may find it closed. The great theologian, C. S. Lewis, felt as if the door to the presence of God was locked and barred on the other side during his grief over the untimely loss of his wife. Lewis remembered Jesus' beatitude, "Blessed are those who mourn, for they shall be comforted" (Matt. 5:4), but it seemed that the only response he received from his pleading for that comfort was silence. It may take a lot longer than you expect to feel any spiritual healing.

If you thought that by living a certain way you would be spared such losses as you have now experienced, **you may feel cheated.** If there is a part of you that believes in an "eye for an eye and a tooth for a tooth," you may wonder what you did to deserve this happening to you. At a time of a major loss in our lives, very primitive religious ideas and fears seem to have a special power. How we react to loss spiritually may in part be related to our experiences growing up or later in life, but it also seems to have something to do with differences in personality.

More will be said about personality type later, but something to keep in mind is that those who have intuition dominant in their personality may exhibit a more positive faith in times of loss than those who prefer a more concrete, "sensing" form of spirituality. For sensing persons, the facts of the situation may add up to feelings of spiritual defeat and abandonment by God. In a later chapter we'll show you how understanding this aspect of your personality may help to alleviate some of the suffering that comes with this kind of thinking.

Understanding personality types has its limits, too. For some things there are no simple solutions. When Job spoke with God after the terrible, horrifying losses he experienced, there was no answer given for his suffering, just the word from his Creator, "Where were you when I laid the foundation of the earth?" And Job answered, "I

know that you can do everything and that no thought can be with-
held from you. Who is he who hides behind counselors without
knowledge? Therefore, I have uttered what I do not understand,
things too wonderful which I do not know" (Job 38, 42).

*Some people, as Job eventually did, place themselves in the hands
of God or a Higher Power with faith and trust, not knowing how
or why things are as they are, but accepting what is. This is not the
same as believing that everything that happens is the "will of God."*

When we think of God as both all-powerful and loving, we have
difficulty knowing how to account for the existence of evil and disaster.
You may see the death of your spouse as an example of this evil.
Rabbi Harold Kushner wrestled with the meaning of suffering and
failed to reconcile the fact with a theology of a loving God, so he
attributed disasters to acts of nature that are beyond the control of
God. Rabbi Kushner's idea may not represent a satisfying solution if
you believe that God is both Creator and in control. Some find their
primary comfort, not in a theory about the relationship of God's love
and God's power, but in a conviction that in everything, God is working for our good, even though we do not understand how that can be
possible in the particular situation of a deeply mourned loss.

*Your doubting and searching for a faith you can apply to your
situation, along with your suffering, is normal.* It is human to
have spiritual questions and even conflicts. It may take several
months before you can feel the presence of a Higher Power again in
your life. It can be hard work to become open to the kind of
spirituality that can handle the stress and trauma of bereavement. Be
assured that it can be done, even without all the answers.

From ancient times comes the strength represented in the following passage: "They who wait for the Lord shall renew their strength,
they shall mount up with wings like eagles; they shall run and not
be weary, they shall walk and not faint" (Isaiah 40:31).

*Passages like this were the basis of the faith by which D Rosalene
lived and died. I heard her say many times, "The Bible says it, I
believe it and that settles it."*

You may not find it easy to maintain such a simple faith during
your time of grief. However, *those who have a reliable spiritual
anchor seem to have increased strength to wrestle with the physical, intellectual and emotional tasks of grief.*

Whatever the source of your feelings, we think that ordinarily the best way to deal with feelings of grief is to permit yourself to experience them and find some caring friend(s), minister, priest or rabbi, counselor or therapist to be with you during the most difficult times. Since not everyone is comfortable around those who are experiencing a strong grief reaction, you need someone who will give you permission to share any of your feelings of grief (whether physical, intellectual, emotional or spiritual) without fear of judgment for as long as it takes for you to purge them from your system. Such people are true friends. This is why many survivors find mutual support groups to be helpful. They are not afraid to witness each other's suffering. May God help you in your search for those who will walk through the valley of the shadow with you.

4

Substitute

Trite as the platitude is, life does go on. The earth still turns, the days come and go, the seasons change and people go about their lives. People get married, babies are born and about four people continue to die every minute. And you live on until it is your turn. While you try to integrate the death of D _____, you must simultaneously learn to live with your loss. To the extent that you have needs and wants that D _____ supplied, you must struggle with their demands and seek their fulfillment or learn to live without. In a marriage relationship, each party plays many roles for the partner. These roles include checkbook balancer, auto repairer, wage earner, cook, housekeeper, lover, lawn mower, challenger, listener, sharer, escort, etc. Some of them are necessary to successful living. Others are nice advantages in marriage but not absolutely necessary for survival. You will need to identify what was absolutely necessary and find ways of accommodating to the primary loss.

William Worden writes about adapting to a world that does not include your loved one. In the beginning of your grief, this may seem impossible. But with time we can learn to adapt to changing circumstances, even in extremely life-threatening situations. Consider the ways that many military people and political prisoners have been able to survive, even with all the suffering they experienced.

In the midst of my grief I became more thankful of my own health when I took greater notice of handicapped people in wheel chairs. One person was missing his entire lower body from the hips down, another person was dwarfed and missing both of her arms. Look around to discover your primary physical, intellectual, emotional and spiritual strengths. Being thankful is not always easy but it is possible.

Abraham Maslow has identified many motivational incentives that people need fulfilled if they are to be happy. He put these needs in order of priority, meaning that the upper level needs are not motivational until the lower level needs are satisfied. At the base of his pyramid are basic physiological survival needs, such as food and shelter. Above these fundamental needs are the needs for safety, then the need for love and a sense of belonging with other people. Then there is the need for self-esteem that comes from within but also through special relationships with significant others. At the upper level of the pyramid of needs is the search for self-fulfillment that he called self-actualization.

Many of these needs can be met in and through a happy marriage and family life. With the loss of the partner who helped supply these needs comes the necessity of finding new ways of recreating them or learning to live without them. The task of Substitution will be helped along if you understand your own personality and set priorities according to your primary unmet needs. You may want to review this chapter after reading what we have to say about personality and loss (Chapter 7).

You can learn to find substitutes for the missing roles of *D* _____, but it will mean learning to go with the flow of your new situation. Take advantage of the opportunities that are presented for a new lifestyle. Resisting the need to adapt will only make the adjustment more difficult and extended. You have been given tremendous resources for adapting to the change that is before you. Whether what is missing is actually replaceable or not, Substitution requires that you overcome your resistance to change and permit yourself to seek and find a new equilibrium.

Physical Substitution (Step 9)

You may be acutely aware of practical physical losses previously supplied by D _____ that can easily be replaced, either by yourself or by family members. Grocery shopping, housecleaning, cooking, possibly child care, etc., are all obvious needs. Widows may be more comfortable with the homemaking aspects of their new life if they were homemakers before their husband's death. Widowers may be more comfortable with the bread-winning aspects of life, the yard upkeep, auto maintenance, investments, etc., if those were the roles they previously filled. Either sex may have to switch over a bit to the roles normally played by their spouse. Some believe this switch may be easier for women than men but others think the opposite.

It may not be so much a gender matter as it is one of prior experience. If your role in the marriage was more traditionally male or female, then assuming the opposite roles may be difficult. *The primary problem at first may be a lack of energy,* coupled perhaps with anxiety about or even a resentful resistance to having to assume the responsibilities formerly handled by your spouse. If this resistance drags on for a while, housekeeping and/or bookkeeping can fall way behind.

In the first few weeks friends, relatives and neighbors may volunteer some help. They may bring in food and offer their personal care. Some may actually do some work but too soon they go back to their own lives, leaving you to fill in the hole that has been left in your life. Then, in addition to the emotional burdens of grief, you will have to find ways of meeting your necessary physical needs as well. However reluctantly, you will eventually learn to do some of the needed chores yourself. You may be able to enlist the aid of volunteers on a continuing basis, or pay for the help needed for other physical needs. Of course — and you know this only too well — some of the physical aspects of your life with D _____ have been eliminated from your new life, forever left behind.

The loss of the physical body contact of your spouse may be very difficult to deal with. Those many years of physical contact cannot easily be replaced, if at all. For many the empty bedroom is far worse to deal with than the empty living room or kitchen.

If you were a sexually active couple, the abrupt loss of your sexual relationship can be very troubling. Sexual relations for some couples are a primary expression of their intimacy. For many others it is closely linked with their feeling of self-esteem. If that was true for you, the lack of D _____'s touch in your life can be one of the most excruciating pains of separation. At first you may recoil from the loss and feel only the acute deprivation of D _____'s physical presence, with no need whatever for sex. After several celibate months, however, your body may again remind you that you are also a sexual person.

Your feeling of physical deprivation may be so acute as to lead you to seek substitute physical contact for your lost intimacy with D _____. This is how some end up in premature relationships with available sexual substitutes. Such relationships sometimes blossom into something more meaningful and lasting, but often they cause additional problems and guilt. They can also generate grief on top of grief, if they break up. Over two-thirds of marriages that occur during recovery from grief end in divorce. At the point where you are considering dating or entering an intimate relationship, ask yourself if you are really ready. *Be aware that too much new emotional investment can complicate your recovery* until you have dealt with the issues involved in Substitution and Detachment (next chapter).

At this stage, there really are only three sexual alternatives: celibacy, masturbation or casual dating encounters. Only you can choose which alternative is right for you at this time. Your intellectual, emotional and spiritual condition will all be involved, in addition to your physical body. If you are active socially, there may be some assertive volunteers who "know what you need" and offer to fill those sexual needs. You will need to guard against such volunteers during your period of greatest vulnerability, since not all offers are as generous as they may seem. Under more normal conditions, you may have been able to sense the motivation of others and protect yourself, if need be. In grief this discretionary sense is dulled. Widows and widowers can sometimes be lured into involvements that are not healthy for them at this time.

Many surviving spouses have found themselves entrapped into a sexually driven relationship before they were intellectually, emotionally or spiritually ready. If you fall into such a trap, the resulting anxiety and guilt can be a major setback in your grief work. *It is not healthy to engage in a sexual relationship purely out of the need for a physical substitute* for D _____. Such single-focus relationships have greater likelihood of being a sign of dependency and attachment hunger at this time. If you are vulnerable, it is easy to get in over your head without understanding what is happening. If compulsive sexual behavior ever becomes a problem for you, recognizing it as a symptom of your need for physical substitution and possibly an attempt to deal with your anxiety and other basic feelings of loss may be the first step in getting it under control. A healthy, active sexual relationship can be a part of reconstruction and will be discussed more fully in the chapter on reconstruction and in the following chapter on relationships. Unless you can renew sexual activity in a nonaddictive, anxiety-free and guilt-free relationship consistent with your personal values, perhaps abstinence is the best course for now. The same can be said about alcohol and other drugs or any type of addictive or compulsive behavior during this time.

Not getting involved in ill-advised sexual relationships, however, does not mean having no physical contact with others. Gary Smalley and John Trent reported research that highlights the importance of physical touch to emotional health. Results of studies at UCLA show that about one-third of all the nerve endings responding to touch exist in the palms of the hands. Helen Colton's research is complementary; the largest area of brain surface responding to touch is devoted to the hand. It is well known that infants who are touched and caressed grow faster and with fewer complications.

Every one of us seems to be born with a need for touch. Researchers reported finding increased production of hemoglobin, the oxygen-carrying substance of the blood, and reduced blood pressure as a direct result of meaningful touch. This research concluded that people need six or more meaningful touches per day or life expectancy could be reduced by two or more years. Touch is clearly one of our most important senses. People can live without sight and hearing, but most newborns do not thrive without touch and we have to wonder if that need does not continue throughout our lives. Helping professionals are being reminded of the role of appropriate touch in the professional practice of medicine, nursing, etc., because it seems to hasten healing.

Because of its sexual connotation, many are uncomfortable with giving or receiving touch, hugs or even holding hands. Perhaps one of the roles that a pet can play for a grieving person is to provide a safe way for some of the normal human "touch" needs to be met. *Having a dog or a cat provides contact with a warm, responsive body that can be therapeutic for many people.*

If your marriage included lots of meaningful touching, the deprivation from that physical loss can be a very significant aspect of your
grief. The physical deprivation can be eased a little by getting nonsexual hugs from people who care about you, but even close friends
and relatives may be reluctant to get that close to you if hugging was
not previously a regular part of your relationship. Now that you are
single, you may also represent a threat to them in some way. You
may need to ask for hugs from those whose physical contact you
want. Be prepared for the possibility that if you make such a request
of an opposite-sex friend, it may be misinterpreted — by others if
not by that person.

Another complication is that, even though you limit yourself to
same sex hugs, unfortunately even a display of light affection between persons of the same sex is often misinterpreted in our sexually liberated society. This may be even more of a problem for men
than for women because Western men traditionally have had less
physical contact with each other, except in athletic activities.

*You may find an acceptable outlet for touch needs at churches
or synagogues or other group gatherings where touch is ritual-
ized.* Some worshipping communities and support groups incorpo-
rate a handshake or hug into their service or as part of a group
opening or closing exercise. Whatever the situation, you will need
to be sensitive to the ego boundaries of others and not force yourself
onto a person who does not seem to be receptive. With some
people, a handshake is about all they have to give but if you are
open to the opportunities, you may find yourself getting healing
hugs more often than you expected.

Masturbation is a private matter in our society. Although studies
indicate that the majority of younger, single people masturbate, its
incidence among older, widowed people is not so well known. James
and Stephen McCary report in *Human Sexuality* that about 59% of
unmarried women between fifty and seventy years of age acknowledge that they masturbate. Throughout the life cycle, the percentage of males who masturbate at different age levels is higher than
the percentage of females who do so. If you never practiced solitary
masturbation during your marriage, it may be difficult for you to
accept this physical substitution now. Masturbation is nevertheless,
one alternative way to meet sexual needs unless there are compelling
religious reasons why you choose not to consider it as an option. You
may find it interesting that one study reported by McCary found no
significant differences in the percentages of males who masturbated
whether they attended church regularly, sometimes or not at all. Of

course, various denominations or religious groups may have specific and strong teachings about different forms of sexual expression.

Underlying these issues is the conflict you may experience between your sexual nature and your own religious beliefs. Many religious leaders advise against sexual activity outside of marriage. While their reasons may appear only to be doctrinal, there is often in their teaching a real concern not only for the sanctity of marriage but also for the dignity of the individual person. However, humans tend to be sexually active so long as there is no physical illness or disability. For those who are "single again," there can be a real dilemma.

To these personal and moral concerns are added today's real dangers, such as AIDS, related to unsafe sexual encounters. Working out a lifestyle that will accommodate your physical needs, your personal values and health concerns may require hard compromise or self-denial. Either way you will probably have some accommodations to make between your physical and spiritual needs in this regard. In this, as in each of the steps of grief, you should do what you believe to be best for you and those close to you, perhaps after consultation with a counselor, keeping in balance the physical, intellectual, emotional and spiritual.

Intellectual Substitution (Step 10)

The intellectual resources you bring to the task of Substitution can be very helpful but they will also meet with frustration as you try to apply logic to the illogical. The relationship you had with D _____ probably included sharing of problems and the mutual search for solutions. Now all your decisions must be made without D _____ and without the benefit of those shared opinions. Substituting your own thoughts may be very difficult for some time if you are depressed. Daniel Wegner showed that, even when positive ideas are offered by external caregivers, deeply depressed people still seem to override them automatically with further negative thoughts, fueling the depression. While you are in this state, there may be friends and relatives who can help with the many problems of living to be solved.

You can also *seek advice of professional counselors* such as a lawyer to draw up or revise your will, a banker or financial advisor to set your banking and investments in order, real estate people to discuss your housing options, an accountant to help with taxes, etc. Support services may be available from your local government agencies and volunteer services to the bereaved. Helpful as they may be, none of them will provide the intimate sharing of problems you experienced with your spouse. You should avoid people who have something to sell until you are thinking clearly. Avoid making any decisions that have far-reaching implications requiring the kind of reasoning you might not be capable of right now. Very little is so important that it cannot be put off for a while, even a year or more, if necessary.

You may find intellectual substitution in grief support groups. If you cannot find one in your area, perhaps you can start one. Contact funeral directors, churches or government agencies to locate others who are recently bereaved. Getting together regularly to share your problems and needs can be a very comforting relationship. Solutions often emerge in such group meetings that do not seem possible when you are wrestling with them alone. Meetings might be arranged in homes of members or in a public place such as a local school or church that might provide free space on a regular basis. You might want to use this book as a guide in your support group discussions. Working your way through these 20 steps of grief while in the company of other survivors may be an effective way to make the most of our approach to recovery. If you can find even one person who will be your personal confidant through the difficult days and months, sharing your feelings, concerns and progress, it will be very beneficial. As mentioned before, look for a chapter of service organizations such as Widowed Persons Service or They Help Each Other Spiritually (THEOS), HOSPICE, government mental health agencies, etc., in your area.

Your inability to share the daily events in your life with D _____ may be a special frustration. You may have been used to discussing current events, work-related activities and dozens of family related topics on a daily basis. Now there may be no one to talk with about those topics, neither the unimportant nor the important, and you may feel alone and abandoned if those times of sharing were important to you. Finding someone to substitute in this role may contribute highly to your future happiness. *You will need to develop new relationships with people in your life who care enough about you to share in the discussion of topics that are important to you.* Begin by listening to those around you and become sensitive to their interests. If you show a real interest in them, you may find those who share your interest and who will become the conversation partners you need in your life.

Unfortunately, some of the sharing of intellectual interests you enjoyed with D _____ is gone forever because no one will be able completely to take *D* _____'s place. You will need to learn how to adapt to a lifestyle without the mental nurturing those intellectual times provided.

This is not as impossible as it may sound at present. In time you can learn to get along on your own if you so choose.

Active inner reflection can become a reasonable substitute for conversation with someone else. For many months the loss of conversation may be part of your deprivation, but eventually you can adapt to being intellectually alone at times. When you are comfortable occasionally substituting silent reflection for conversation, you will be on the road to recovery. Then you can begin the task of reconstruction.

Emotional Substitution (Step 11)

Loss of emotional intimacy may be one of the more difficult needs to meet after the death of your spouse. As we noted earlier, clinical professionals in a wide variety of disciplines agree on a critical linkage between intimacy and mental health. Some of the deepest sources of satisfaction in life come with intimate ties to spouse, children, friends, etc.

If your spouse was your closest friend, a substitute for that role in your life may be important to your adjustment. Research at Loyola University of Chicago reported by McAdams and Bryant in the *Journal of Personality,* September 1987, has shown that women associate intimacy with greater happiness and gratification, whereas men associate intimacy with lack of strain and lack of uncertainty. These findings support the idea that a capacity for close and warm interpersonal relationships contributes to mental health and a sense of well-being but the reasons why that is true are different for men than they are for women.

Women living alone who possess high needs for intimacy reported lower levels of gratification and more uncertainty in their lives. *The need for intimacy seems to decline significantly over the life span for women while it may actually increase for men.* This trend could support the theory posed by Carl G. Jung in which he claimed that men and women tend to adopt roles and orientations characteristic of the opposite sex as they move from young to middle adulthood. Jung felt that the feminine part of man, the anima, and the masculine part of woman, the animus, needed to become more developed as the person became older if the person was to become more healthily individuated. If what Jung thought is true, it is understandable that research would suggest some change in both males and females in regards to needs for emotional intimacy.

High intimacy contributes to a woman's overall happiness and satisfaction with life, while for men it makes for less strain in life, fewer emotional symptoms and greater sense of certainty. Intimacy may help women to define their self-image in terms of relationships with other people. Warm, close, communicative relationships may provide men with self-assurance, confidence and security. Such ties may enable the man to venture out into the world, much as the infant needs a secure base to explore the world. Therefore, low intimacy may be expected to lead to greater levels of anxiety, immobility, strain and even physical health problems for men as indirect signs of lack of support for the self in interpersonal relations. For women intimacy may function less as a secure base and more in the manner of providing a sense of identity through which the concept of self may be built up.

Carefully assess your need for intimacy and, just as carefully, begin to reach out to new single friends as well as old friends and relations for this need. Unfortunately for some survivors, this need will be difficult to meet unless new relationships are developed. Women may find this reaching out easier to do than men and those with extraverted personalities may find it easier than those who are introverted.

It is possible that, in your emotionally vulnerable state, *you may have the opportunity and the inclination to become involved in addictive behavior of one sort or another* as a form of substitution. This could take many forms, such as addiction to medication, food, TV, alcohol, drugs and even "love" and sex. If your emotional substitute becomes compulsive and destructive, you may need counseling to help you break free of it. Volunteer support groups such as Alcoholics Anonymous, Al-Anon, Sex and Love Addicts Anonymous, Co-dependents Anonymous, and other 12-step programs are available in most large cities. We urge you to seek such help if needed. If in doubt, our suggestion is that you attend a few such meetings to evaluate their possible contribution to your adjustment.

Emotional responses to the task of substituting involve your feeling that all this should not really be necessary. Emotional responses could involve the continuing denial of your loss of D _____ and/or a feeling of resentment or rage that you are going through any of this at all. When you are in a crisis, you naturally want to have the burden of stress lifted from your shoulders in some way. *You may strike out in anger or hostility at those who offer the very help that you need.* They may feel hurt and turn away from you if they misunderstand your reactions and take personally your lashing out. This is a time for open communication. Your personality may make it difficult to share your feelings with other people, but only in emotional sharing will you be able to find those in your life who are truly able to accept you as you are and who will become or remain real, intimate friends.

It is necessary for you to let your helpers know how you feel emotionally. Since you can no longer share your feelings with your spouse it may be helpful to share them with the new friends in your life. This may be a reliable way of testing the commitment and motives of those who approach you. If they are not frightened away by your emotional needs, they may become a friend indeed but do not be too surprised if they do not understand and think you are ungrateful for the help they are offering.

To avoid misunderstandings, *it is important to express your appreciation for all the help you do get.* You need not weigh each favor in terms of its value, nor do you need to return every favor. If possible and appropriate, an informal note of thanks may be a helpful relationship builder. At this time of your life, it may be necessary for you to practice receiving graciously. Remember that although it may be more blessed to give than to receive, it takes gracious receivers to make it possible for others to give. If your role in your relationship with D _____ was mostly giving, this new role of graciously receiving may be something that requires a little more sensitivity on your part than you actually feel like at this time. Every burden that someone else helps you to carry is that much less stress that you must deal with. As your helpers realize their emotional support and aid are appreciated, they may be more inclined to provide continuing aid and support.

You may fear that you will not be able to make the substitutions or make the necessary adaptations to maintain your life. If people keep at it, with a little help from others, most of those who have experienced a significant loss are able to discover that they have the emotional resources to get them through.

Spirituality And Substitution (Step 12)

Spiritual aid in your task of Substitution may come from traditional resources (your church, synagogue, etc.). But sometimes even those who have a religious resource to draw upon may find those to whom they look for help are unsure how best to help.

Ministers, rabbis and other spiritual leaders are generally well trained to respond to situations of loss at the beginning, when a death occurs and through the time of the funeral. Later, when the tasks of grief are different, sometimes these caring persons just do not know exactly how to help. Religious communities often are oriented toward those who are couples with families, so the single person may have a harder time feeling that he or she fits.

You may find yourself wondering if you need to have a new or different spiritual "home." *Since major changes of any kind are not recommended for those in this period of grief,* our encouragement is for you to try to find the support you need within your present spiritual framework. Remember that a part of the pain of this time is that D _____ is not with you. What seems like a lack in your spiritual environment may in part be your realization that here is another area of your life with D _____ that is over.

Sometimes what is not available in one congregation or religious setting is available through clusters of congregations, synagogues, etc. For example, some Roman Catholic Dioceses have "Single Again" groups to which members from any parish can go, including visitors from other denominations. Religious leaders and grief counselors ordinarily know what might be available in the wider community that combines emotional support with spiritual sensitivity.

Whatever it takes, *attend to what any 12-Step Program acknowledges as a basic need: the recognition that we need more power than we can consciously bring to some situations* if there is to be ultimate health and healing. Some battles we really do not have to fight alone. We can rely on the most powerful ally of all if we can but open our personal boundaries and let our Higher Power flow through us and become an integrating reality in our lives.

This is also time to *become more sensitive to your intuition,* which we believe is the window to our spiritual resources in time of grief. Our experience suggests that people approach spiritual issues in various ways according to their personalities. As we shall see more fully later on, people have different personality preferences for perceiving and deciding. Those who prefer Sensing perception may look to the works of nature in the physical universe for a glimpse of God; those who prefer Thinking may approach the issue from an intellectual, philosophical pathway; and those who prefer Feeling will search for peaceful harmony and service to mankind.

Those who rely on Intuitive perception and who learn to use it may be able to experience a special kind of spiritual support during this time. Lew says it this way: *I became more sensitive to my inner voice at first awakening in the morning, during that brief time before I became fully conscious and aware of my body. Others may find the window to their subconscious is more open at various times of meditation, such as bedtime or midday. The important thing is to become open to windows to the subconscious that may provide the spiritual comfort that you need. Make some time in your day, every day, to get into a quiet place of meditation and let your spirit commune with the spirit of its creator.*

In the previous section on feelings, we described the spiritual loss that may come about through the loss of intimacy. How does one create a substitute for the loss of spiritual intimacy? It is difficult to offer specific suggestions that will be just right for you. Each person approaches his need for spiritual intimacy somewhat differently because we have different needs, cultural backgrounds and values. This may be a time to become more intuitively aware of the possibility of spiritual gifts and to be open to accepting them when they are presented. You can become a gracious receiver of the spiritual gifts and thereby permit others to receive the blessings that only come with giving. Such spiritual gifts can be presented in the form of physical, intellectual, emotional or more traditionally religious sharing. They may come from the least expected sources at the least expected times under the least expected circumstances. Don't try to analyze the whys and wherefores too much because life includes a place for mystery. Not everything fits neatly in the categories of time and space. When you recognize that spiritual gifts have come, receive them with thankfulness and enjoy their benefits to your life.

5

Detach

There may be a time past that you now wish could have been frozen for eternity but that is not possible, as you know. There is no static utopia, only process, movement, change and development on the road to becoming someone new and different. Life does not remain as is and we must either move on with it or regress; our only choices are growth or decay. We cannot preserve the present or the past, no matter how desirable or painful either one might be.

The continuing process of life requires that you must put the past behind you and move on into your future. *To detach means to give up your physical, intellectual, emotional and spiritual investment in your past* with D_____. It demands that you confront your protest, denial, anxiety, anger, fear and guilt and overcome them. It means you must confront any attachment hunger or co-dependence and overcome that too. It means you will have to internalize your loss of *D* _____ and allow your loved one to become a part of you in a new way. You must let go of the physical, intellectual, emotional and spiritual life you shared with *D* _____. This withdrawal may be made possible by following a process that helps people let go. It begins by releasing all the emotions attached to the memory of *D* _____ that keep you living in the past. This task can be excruciatingly painful and lonely, but it is by letting go of what ties us to the past that a future becomes possible.

In addition, detaching means that you will need to let go of all the "shoulds" that may now crowd into your consciousness. What life could (and should) have been like with *D* _____ is no longer relevant. The feeling that you should not be suffering this loss at this time of your life also is irrelevant. The fact is that you are. *Until and unless you can purge your thinking of how life should now be or could have been, it will be difficult to detach and go on.* Confronting and demolishing the twin emotions of anger and guilt over this reaction may be extremely difficult and energy consuming.

As with all the other tasks, no one can set the timing for detaching but you. However, without finishing this task, the process of reconstruction will always be stunted. New relationships may be substitutes instead of new, independent situations. By "finishing" we do not mean total completion. This task, like all the others, may never be fully completed. Remember our earlier illustration of walking half the distance from where you are to a wall. No matter how many times you do it, the complete task is still there before you. You do get closer with each trip, and eventually the remaining distance is small enough to ignore. But it is still there. .

None of the tasks of untimely grief are easy, but if we had to choose the toughest one, we would select detaching. The reason is that detachment from the past leaves you floating in space and time without any security if your future is not as certain as your past. "Hanging on" may provide a false form of security that protects us from the anxiety of a fearful and uncertain future.

Detachment requires letting go of the security blanket. It is like hanging onto a precipice over a rocky cliff. It may not be very comfortable but it seems safer than letting go. You are like a trapeze flyer who has let go of the bar and is spinning in air, reaching out but not yet connecting with your partner — suspended in time and space at the point of highest risk.

Erich Lindemann said that *detaching is the process of extricating yourself from your bondage to the deceased and finding new patterns of rewarding human interaction and social support* to bolster your self-esteem. The more intimately you were bonded to your spouse and the more dependent upon D _____ you were for your self-esteem, the more difficult will be this task of detachment. The loss of security you enjoyed in your marriage can now become a millstone around your neck that threatens to pull you under the waves of grief and submerge you in a sea of suffering. You can continue your life in the attached state, along with the pain of physical separation, up to the limits of your endurance. You can decide to remain exclusively attached to your dead spouse for the rest of your life but you must be aware that you will be substituting a dead spouse for the live one you lost. If you make that choice, you will be ruling out any blessings that may be waiting for you in new relationships.

In the process of dealing with this choice, you may encounter seasons of ambivalence — part of you trying to detach and part of you wanting to hang on. It is very difficult to give up the idealized security of the past for the uncertainty and risk of the future. You may also feel that D _____ is trying to hold onto you. Coping with those feelings may consume oceans of energy and you may again feel that your coping limits have been exceeded. If you want to obtain healing, you will need to let go and free yourself from the past relationship with D _____ in order to go on to a healthy reconstruction. Wouldn't D _____ not only want you to remember the past but also to be happy in the life you now must lead?

The task of detaching might be eased somewhat if you were able to do some anticipatory grieving. Therese Rando and others explained the role of anticipatory grief in spousal bereavement. If the death of your spouse came after a long illness that provided adequate warning, both of you may have been able to prepare for the loss to follow. While you began your grief process as you thought about your coming loss, D _____ was also experiencing grief over the approaching loss of life and ultimate separation from you. If this process of anticipatory grief was not well managed, neither of you were adequately prepared for the task of detachment that now confronts you. If you did not have time for anticipatory grief due to sudden death, or if you denied the impending death, then detachment may also be more difficult.

Whether the loss was expected or not, if we did not let go before death occurs, then we must let go during this task of detachment if we are going to recover fully from the loss. Now let's look at the resources that you have available for this task.

Physical Detachment (Step 13)

John Bowlby observed that hospitalized young children separated from their mothers moved from "protest" to "despair" to "detachment." In the protest stage, babies will scream, make frantic attempts to get away or attempt to regain the lost mother. In despair, they will weep and act increasingly hopeless. Finally, they will detach and become more sociable with the nurses and neighboring patients. If this phase is completed, babies will be listless and turn away when the parent returns. If detachment is not complete, babies will revert to frantic clinging when the mother returns. The feelings of security are linked to the beloved mother and her presence is needed to maintain a sense of well-being. But if detachment is completed, this need is no longer dominant. So it is with bereaved spouses.

Detaching yourself from the physical presence of your spouse may seem to be impossible for a long time but with D _____'s death you are now detached physically. You may wish it were not so, but there it is. The deprivation you feel from the loss of D _____'s body and personality may be excruciating if you had a close physical union in your relationship. No more touch, no more voice, no more sex, no more sharing, no more . . .

Your physical detachment from D _____ will be a critical sensory experience. You must pick up or touch the physical possessions left behind and dispose of them in an appropriate manner. This can be very difficult to do and you may not be ready to do it for a while. Disposing of things too soon may not be the best idea but resisting it too long also is not helpful in the grief process. No matter when you do it, you may feel that you are desecrating a sacred temple. Many survivors live in a shrine dedicated to the memory of the lost one. Removing or disposing of its contents may seem like an unfaithful thing to do. So the personal garment remains on the hook, the ring on the dresser, the family pictures on the wall.

The intensity of the feeling that nothing should be touched usually diminishes with time, making it easier to let go of these personal possessions. When the time comes, perhaps you can make sure that children or other significant persons have the opportunity to select

from what you no longer need. Then it might help if you find someone who was not closely attached to D _____ to
help you store or dispose of the remainder.

William Worden divided the personal possessions of the deceased
into three groups. **Keepsakes** are items that become softly comforting because of the place they carry in your memory. They are nice
to have around the house and you will probably want to pass on
such things as family pictures, scrapbooks, valuable souvenirs and
the like to the children or heirs, if any. Their loss would not be
devastating but they do have tremendous sentimental value. **Linking
items** are possessions that keep you attached to your spouse. These
are not easy to part with because they feed your co-dependent
attachment hunger. If you are not able to dispose of them after a
reasonable time, your behavior may indicate that you are stuck in
this task and will be unable to move on until you overcome that
attachment. **Transitional items** are those possessions that are part
of your process of growing. They become less important to you
with time and as you make the detachment, they will be easier to
dispose of, especially if others might be able to use them.

Personal project materials, such as sewing, reading, crafts, etc.,
may be distributed to people who can use them as soon as you are
ready to do so. The same goes for clothing. Privately personal items
such as makeup, underwear, lingerie, etc., might best be discarded,
hard as that may be.

Jointly used household goods are something else. Although you
may no longer need them, such items might be retained for future
use by your children or donated to needy people in the community.
They will be a constant reminder of the past and if their presence
is still painful after a year or so, you should consider replacing
them with new furnishings, if possible. If your spouse made all the
home decorating decisions, you may consider redecorating to suit
your own taste as well. That way, you will be reclaiming the living
space that you shared with D _____ as your
own. Gradually, "our place" will become "my place." Just as gradually, "we" becomes "I."

Items that have market value may be donated to a suitable charity,
whether you choose to itemize them for tax deductions or not. The
feeling that D _____ is helping others in this
way may be a comfort to you.

Of course, none of these changes comes easily. The process of
physical detachment presents the most tangible evidence that your
life with D _____ is over. Hard as it may be,

your mental health may require that you make the physical separation real in a tangible way as soon as you can, removing the linking objects first, the transitional objects next and making a space in your life for the remaining keepsake items. Otherwise, you may get stuck in denial or protest and actually find it more difficult to break free as time goes by. Again, as with the other tasks of grief, if this step seems dreadfully hard to take we suggest that you seek professional help in getting on with it.

Intellectual Detachment (Step 14)

The intellectual detachment from D _____ will test your rational thinking. While it may seem quite logical that the intellectual acknowledgment of death should be followed naturally by the intellectual detachment, that is easier said than done. The mind rebels at change which it does not want to accept. The thinking person is shocked when the rational thinking process that we have learned to trust throughout our life now fails to meet our needs.

You may continue to be affected by the inability of reason to give you a satisfactory answer to your ongoing question, a universal question: "Why?" If you cannot shake the question, it adds additional heaviness to the burden of grief. Along with the continuing question, you may sometimes surprise yourself, even at this stage, with how unreal it seems that D _____ is gone. This sense of unreality is a defense mechanism that helps you tolerate the suffering. It goes with denial, which comes and goes but you know by now that D _____ is not coming back.

To assist in this process of detachment, it may be helpful to review the memories of your life with D _____. Begin with your original meeting and develop a chronological account of your married life together. You might want to record your recollections on a tape recorder or write them down in a journal. Be sure to include an account of the final illness and death of your spouse. Reviewing the memories of those times and the event itself will not be easy but it can be helpful.

Keeping a journal or diary of your grief process can also be helpful. When you look back on it, you will be able to see the progress that may not be obvious to you as you go through the process of grief. Not sensing any progress usually leads to more frustration and pain than is necessary. It may be a good idea to keep such a journal for at least two years.

For whatever length of time you might choose to refer to
D _____ as your wife or husband is another
choice you will have to make. Some find that when they begin
referring to the one they lost by first name only, they were helping
themselves acknowledge even more the fact of the death. This way
of speaking also may be a way of affirming their own independent
identity. However, others may choose to continue referring to "my
wife" or "my husband" until they choose to let go of their married
role. The most important issue is whether or not you are detaching
in such a way that enables you to be open to your personal future.

Your marriage may have provided opportunities for enhancing your self-esteem through a sense of acceptance, approval,
love, achievement, etc. Now the loss of your relationship with
D _____ may also result in loss of self-esteem
if it was dependent upon the reflected image you received from
your mate. David Burns offers four rational solutions to a loss of
self-esteem based on addictive, co-dependent attachment to what
somebody else gives us. *First* is accepting the idea that your worth
is not and never was based on achieving any abstract "things." The
second concept is that whatever our "worth," each human being
has an equal share of it from birth until death. *Third,* you can only
lose your sense of self-worth by persecuting yourself mentally with
negative, unreasonable, illogical thoughts. *Fourth,* self-esteem is
actually based on a decision to treat yourself with love, respect and
the same approval you would grant a VIP or beloved friend. You do
not have to earn the right to treat yourself in this caring way. You
already have that right but you may have to detach from the illogical
forms of thinking that make you feel less of a person now that you
are single and alone again. If it is holding back your recovery, it will
be helpful to detach from this negative form of thinking about your
self-worth. You can then escape from the trap of believing that your
self-esteem was ever really based on acceptance, approval, love
and achievement as part of your relationship with
D _____. We do not claim it is easy but it
certainly is desirable for the sake of your peace of mind.

Emotional Detachment (Step 15)

The emotional attachment to your spouse may be very difficult to
break. When D _____ died, *you may have felt
abandoned.* You may also be left with what Howard Halpern called
an "attachment hunger." *Attachment hunger is explained as an*

emotional addiction to another person. It is a form of co-dependence that is widely recognized as the condition that ensues when a
lover who is separated languishes, mopes and pines for the beloved.

The lovesick mind becomes distracted from its normal commitments and becomes preoccupied with desire and longing for the
beloved. The person deeply in love becomes addicted to the love
partner, obsessed and preoccupied with the next "fix" of being together, talking, loving, relating in the closest form of intimacy. This
kind of emotional dependence has some psychological similarities to
the addictive behavior of the drug addict and usually requires a painful,
lengthy process of recovery. Addictive, co-dependent behavior usually
has roots deep in childhood and dysfunctional families. It can best be
understood with professional help or by participating in the rapidly
growing 12-step method of support provided through local groups of
Co-dependents Anonymous (CODA) or Al-Anon or ACoA.

Halpern defined attachment hunger as a hangover from the early
time in your childhood when you were not a viable person without
being connected to your mother. It may result in a dependency in
adult human relationships as one tries to replace the former relationship with the dysfunctional parents. If you were never encouraged
to become an independent person by your dysfunctional parents,
getting married may be an attempt to obtain an idealized relationship. If you did not get the kind of parenting you needed, you may
seek it in your adult relationships. *Over the years the marriage
relationship may have become based more on emotional dependence than on interdependent love.* Death abruptly severs the
relationship and thrusts the survivor back into infantile or adolescent
acute loneliness, bred of the dependency.

The more you can accept that you are now a separate, adequate
and complete person, the less you will need to be victimized by the
infantile feeling that you must be attached to someone in order to
survive physically, intellectually, emotionally and spiritually. The
stronger your sense of having your own unique, complete identity,
the less subject you will be to being controlled by your co-dependent
attachment hunger. If that sense of personal identity is not well
developed, your task of detachment will be much more difficult and
prolonged. So if these descriptions apply to you, you may need to
explore the addictive, co-dependent aspect of your personality and
deal with this issue before you move into reconstruction.

If your family of origin was dysfunctional for reasons of alcohol
or drug addiction, chronic illness, or other social reasons that inter-
fered with parenting, you may have grown into a co-dependent

Adult Child who relied unconsciously on your marriage relationship to meet some deep dependency needs. Only recently have the effects of faulty lifestyles during childhood been recognized as a leading and pervasive cause of the development of co-dependent people. Some estimates have suggested there is a very high rate of co-dependency among adults. It is not surprising that mental health agencies are beginning to offer specific co-dependent treatment programs to meet the burgeoning need.

So long as your co-dependent needs were being met in your marriage, you may not have been aware of having this problem in your life. In fact, the circumstances surrounding the death of D _____ may have passed this dysfunction along to your own children. Now the need to address your own unmet dependency needs may be brought to light, demanding attention and keeping you attached to the relationship that has ended. If you suspect this is so, reading the books by Melody Beattie, Charles Whitfield, Anne Wilson Schaef and Pia Mellody will help you learn more about your needs.

Some of the symptoms of co-dependency include:

- Steadfast loyalty, even when it is unjustified or harmful
- The need to be needed in order to have a relationship with others
- Tendency to put the needs of others before our own
- Judging everything we do by the standards of other people
- Self-esteem based on reflections from others — being unable to acknowledge good things about ourselves
- Letting others determine what we say and do
- Difficulty making decisions
- Fear of being hurt or rejected by others
- Difficulty identifying and expressing our feelings
- Assuming responsibility for the behavior and feelings of others.

If there is a recognition of this problem in your community, chances are that volunteer support groups may be available for people like yourself to attend. The telephone company may help to find them under the heading of Co-dependents Anonymous (CODA) or Al-Anon or ACoA. Modeled after the 12-step programs of chemical addictions, such group meetings are attracting rapidly growing numbers of people all over the country. If you cannot find one,

contact the national center of Co-dependents Anonymous at the
address listed in Gary's *Afterword.*

*In therapy I learned that being the first-born to dysfunctional
parents (my parents lost their first baby at birth), my teenage years
were spent in being a substitute "husband" for my mother. I did
adult household chores and helped her to keep house since she was
chronically ill and a housebound recluse. My father was absent,
working most of the time and when he was home he was a perfectionistic taskmaster. I sacrificed my own pleasure pursuits as I became a caretaker and prematurely assumed adult responsibilities
of homemaking, never learning how to play. When I was accepted
into the family of my wife, I perceived an opportunity to escape my
own dysfunctional home life but I took with me the co-dependent
role I had been taught. After the loss of my wife, it became necessary
to give up that role and begin to look after my own needs, a new
role that nothing in my experience had prepared me to do.*

Breaking free of the addiction to attachment hunger may require that you literally go back to your childhood, emotionally
speaking. You need to learn what you did not learn then, or learned
but forgot over the many years of emotional dependence: how to be
an emotionally independent, whole adult. Useful measures that have
been offered by Halpern and Whitfield include turning inward to
the "I am" messages within you, becoming more aware of your own
physical body, employing fantasy and meditation to contact the inner
you, relearning what you really want from life, practicing the intentional stoppage of negative thoughts about your loss to help get
over the relationship that has ended, connecting with the timeless
aspect of life through the wonders of nature and purposefully seeking your own growth and development. This often can be best done
with professional help in therapy.

Genuine love also poses a problem of emotional detachment.
You may have been used to giving your love and all its commitment
to your spouse. You gave yourself to D _____
and now you must detach in order to go on. This is what Scott Peck
calls "decathecting." It is the opposite process of the cathecting that
took place when you fell in love at first. Then it was more or less
involuntary; now it must be purposefully voluntary.

D. Phillips offers several behavioral techniques intended to help
you intentionally get over a relationship that has ended. There is a
time to think about it and a time not to think about it. To continue

to obsessively think about it after you understand it and have the knowledge to strengthen your identity as a separate person serves no further constructive purpose. At that point, it makes sense to use whatever techniques may be helpful to end the preoccupation and free yourself. If your love is genuine, you should eventually be able to let D _____ go in a way that enables you to go on with your life.

Detaching certainly does not mean that you need to stop loving D _____. In fact, you can choose to continue loving your spouse the rest of your life, along with many other people who deserve your love. We can love more than one person at a time. But we cannot love them all with equal commitment and responsibility. You are no longer married to D _____ so the degree of responsibility and commitment you retain is totally of your own choosing. *So long as you choose to be totally committed to D* _____, *you will not be able to develop a new relationship of the same intensity with the same degree of commitment and responsibility to anybody else.* As with all the other tasks of grief, the choice is yours, and only you can tell when you are ready to make it. And as with the other tasks, it may be hard work, but the payoff in peace of mind is well worth the effort.

There is also the need to detach yourself from the emotions of grief that may have consumed you. Letting go of the fear, the anxiety, the anger, the jealousy, the guilt and the depression also demands great energy and a conscious effort of will. So long as you permit these emotions to persist, they may create a bitterness and self-pity that can only retard your healing. Until they are purged, you can be stuck in the feeling task of grief. The potential for full enjoyment of the life that remains for you may be diminished or even completely choked off. What you do about this is a choice that you can make, _____. As described elsewhere in this book, cognitive therapy may help you make this emotional adjustment. It is especially helpful in letting go of any anxiety, anger and guilt that may be keeping you stuck in this task. Books by David Barlow and Jerome Cerny and those by Gary Emery and David Burns will be helpful if you teach yourself to apply the techniques they recommend to help reorient your beliefs and thinking which generate your feelings and emotions. Or you might check to see what counseling resources are available in your area that use the cognitive therapy principles.

Since our culture does not encourage the open expression of grief feelings, as some others do, it is harder to let feelings run their course so we can detach from them. Letting them go also means we give up our ties to the comfortable past that no longer exist and step into the future with all its risk and uncertainty. It is not an easy thing to do. It is tempting just to remain attached to the past through your memories and fantasies, even though you may develop new, substitute relationships.

One of the most difficult aspects of detachment may be the resolution of what Elisabeth Kubler-Ross and others have called *"unfinished business."* This means letting go of all the personal issues that were left uncompleted between you and your spouse. In fact, the whole program of grief recovery advocated by John James and Frank Cherry concentrates on the identification and resolution of such outstanding issues with the deceased. They advocate not only thinking about such issues but also writing them down and talking them through with a "grief partner" in a detailed 16-step procedure.

Their process is divided into three phases. *In the first phase you recall and share with your grief partner all the losses of your life,* including pets, relocations, deaths, etc., and try to pin down what the experiences taught you about grieving. You probably learned to bury your feelings, replace the loss, grieve alone, just give it time, regret the past, and avoid trusting to avoid further pain. These are all erroneous beliefs that can keep you from honestly communicating your grief to those closest to you.

In the second phase you recall and share with your grief partner all the main positive and negative events that occurred in your life with the deceased partner, and what you did or did not do in the circumstances. This helps identify all the incomplete aspects of the relationship and what you did or did not do to make it incomplete.

In the final phase, you communicate with your grief partner all the undelivered messages you now wish could have been resolved with your lost loved one. These include positive things that were not acknowledged, negative things that were not resolved, and things you wished you could have said but didn't. In this phase, you must be willing to acknowledge your role in not having communicated these things to your loved one and then let go. It is important not to be self-critical; people usually do the best they can under the circumstances and so do loved ones. The main emotional areas in which we are usually incomplete are making amends for things we are sorry for having said or done, or not having said or done; offering forgiveness for real or imagined grievances against the beloved and expressing emotional statements of love, pride, etc.

The final act in the process of letting go can be writing a letter to D _____ and reading it to your grief partner, as though your loved one were actually there. Be as truthful as possible about all the unfinished business and then say goodbye and destroy the letter. James and Cherry believe this method is worth trying if you are having difficulty letting go. Of course, it must be done with complete trust and confidentiality. Because of the issues that may surface, we recommend that your grief partner be a trained grief counselor.

We all have uncompleted relationships with everyone we know. And no matter how much time you may have had to prepare yourself for this ultimate separation, chances are you did not resolve all your differences or open-ended issues. They are especially, acutely painful now because there is no longer any hope of reconciliation or compromise, at least in this life. You must live with the uncompleted issues, whether they are insignificant or monumental. Living in this situation can be excruciatingly painful. So it is important to try to come to some resolution unilaterally on the open-ended matters that still exist between you and D _____.

If you cannot do this by yourself, or with the help of a surrogate as proposed by James and Cherry, professional help may well be worth the investment. You must identify all the open issues that inhibit your healing and find ways of dealing with them so you can come to some form of personally satisfactory closure. Forgiving yourself and D _____ for any unresolved grievances that may still exist is very difficult but necessary to achieving some acceptable peace of mind.

Lewis B. Smedes wrote about the importance of forgiveness in maintaining mental health. We mentioned briefly earlier in this book that you may be hurting from the anger you feel toward your dead spouse for leaving you. Smedes observed that *the process of forgiveness needed to release yourself* from this pain flows through four stages.

The first is a crisis stage of feeling the hurt. Second comes the rage or hatred that is directed at the person who hurt you so. Third, there comes a form of healing when you forgive someone for hurting you. You perform a sort of surgery inside your soul, cutting away the wrong that was done to you so you can see your dead spouse through new eyes. You can detach from the hurt and the rage and let them go, reversing the seemingly irreversible flow of pain within you. Finally, there is a stage of renewal as you take in the lost spouse in a new way — continuing to love, but no longer feeling the hurt.

Such forgiving is love's remedy for the unfair treatment life has handed us through this separation from the one to whom our total, exclusive commitment may have meant our very existence.

If you have not reached a comfortable emotional detachment in a year or two with the support of friends and relatives, perhaps more professional counseling would then be helpful. Seeking such help is nothing to be ashamed of and it is never too late to try and free yourself from the bondage of such grief attachments. Some people have entered counseling more than a decade after the death of their spouse. It is better to confront your pain and get it over with in a timely manner. If you need professional help, just remember that you are worth it!

Spirituality And Detachment (Step 16)

You may not have been conscious of it but over the time you spent with D _____ there occurred a spiritual bonding as well as a physical, intellectual and emotional bonding. You may have enjoyed the spiritual intimacy described by Patrick and Thomas Malone that enabled you to know your true self in the presence of your spouse. Now this aspect of your relationship must also take its place in your past.

Perhaps it is only as you can detach yourself spiritually that you may become a whole, single person again. Some religious views hold that after death people will be able to identify and know each other but there is no agreement on whether relationships are expected to be the same as in earthly marriage.

One view is that, while we may all be together collectively with loved ones, the oneness may be universal and not paired one to one. The realization of this state of being will be joyous, although contemplating it may cause a mixture of anticipation and dread over the loss of unrecoverable physical communion with loved ones as we have known it.

In some contemporary movements, the idea of reincarnation seems to be in vogue. It suggests people may have the opportunity of reuniting with their loved ones in some future life together, just as your past marriage may have been a reunion of a relationship from a previous life. Within Christian communities, it is not uncommon for people to believe that the loved one is waiting for them, along with other relatives and family members, to rejoin the union in the presence of God. Many Christians hope for a promised res-

urrection of the body and a new heaven and a new earth in which
all sadness, sickness and separation will be banished.

As with love, *detachment does not mean spiritual disconnection.*
So do not be surprised if you always experience a sense of spiritual
connection to D _____. Even as you detach, it
can be a source of comfort and healing to know the security of the
bond that still exists.

Spiritual relationships are one of the mysteries of the universe.
Those who find themselves having difficulty going on, not because
they don't want to go on but because they don't know how to let go,
may find the following visualization worth considering:

*A mental exercise I was taught by a healer to help me make this
difficult spiritual release may be helpful to you. While you recite the
following words, visualize D _____ encased in
a transparent balloon illuminated by heavenly light that you hold in
your cupped hands before you. Release it upward as you permit
D _____ to ascend into heaven. Repeat this ex-
ercise whenever you feel that attachment hunger is prohibiting the
release that D _____ needs in order to go on
with life in the spiritual plane. Recite these following words. You can
do this exercise at any time and in any place. If in public, you may
want to recite the verse silently but if you are alone, saying it aloud
will be beneficial.*

D _____, I love you.

D _____, I bless you.

D _____, I release you to your highest good.

*You may feel the need to repeat this visual image many times.
You will know when the need to recite this exercise becomes less and
less with longer gaps in between. Some day it may no longer be
necessary.*

When your task of detachment is accomplished well enough, you
will be ready to undertake the task of Reconstruction. But you still
must recognize that the various tasks of grief may never be completely finished. They are now a permanent part of your life. You will
be working on them as long as you live. You can put them away for
a while but they will assert their demands on your conscious mind
whenever an event or encounter reminds you of your loss. It may be
a song, a look at the moon, a smell or any type of sensory stimulation that triggers your grief again and again. Instantly, you will be
involved in one or more of these tasks. If you can recognize when

these events occur and identify the challenge of grief that applies at the moment, it may make your process a little easier as time goes by.

In case you have been wondering about it, that little verse about the moon on the opening page of the Introduction is one D Rosalene taught me after we were engaged, to recite with her at identical times of the day near bedtime when we were separated during the first year of our marriage. She had gone back to college to finish her last year and I returned for my final year of Air Force duty. Knowing that each of us was reciting the same poem at the same time helped us to maintain some level of intimacy during the enforced separation. For the first year or so after she died, I could not bear to look up at the moon at all. Now I cannot look at the moon without recalling her and those exquisite times of our lives. But it is no longer as painful for me to do so. I felt like sharing our private poem with you.

6

Reconstruct

In this chapter, we treat the transition from grieving to being widowed, from being married to being single again. This is a time for adaptation to change. Your devastation may be overwhelming for some time, maybe even several years. Your social, cultural and psychological makeup, based on years of experience and role modeling, may have fixed you in a pattern of maintaining a nuclear family, with your spouse playing a central role in your life. As one husband said about his wife after a 40-year marriage, "I made the living and she made the living worthwhile." Now that relationship is ended. You must construct a new life based on facts that are different from your traditional way of looking at life. This is a time to redirect your behavior and activities toward meeting your own needs. Place your name on the line that follows, as a reminder that the focus in Reconstruction

is not on *D* _____ but on *you* (your name)
_____.

Like it or not, you are now forced to recreate a new life as a single person in a rapidly changing culture. The traditional American family of working father, non-working mother and two or three children is rapidly disappearing. In its place, there is appearing a variety of more independent and sometimes temporary forms of human relationships that you are now thrust into.

For months I awoke each morning in fear and panic with the thought, "My God, she is gone and I am alone." Sometime during the second year, I began to wake up with the thought, "My God, she is gone and I am free." (I did not want to be free.) True reconstruction may only begin when you can awake with the thought, "Thank you, God, I am finally free." I had not yet reached this state after 36 months.

Then the possibility of freedom gradually started to become real for me. But it took until the end of the fourth year for me to consciously begin wondering what I would do with my new freedom. Still, I could not work out a plan for my life with any degree of confidence. I could not figure out what I really wanted, much less what was best for me. I felt like I was walking around in the rubble of a demolished building that was my life. I was numb, in shock and disbelief, caught in a world of unreality. During the three years of D Rosalene's illness, my two children also grew into independence. My daughter moved clear across the country to the opposite coast. In therapy I learned that I was programmed to be a "good daddy," "good husband" and "good son." All those roles, which had driven my life for over 50 years, were gone and I was left with a complete rebuilding job. Talk about your empty nest mid-life crisis!

The untimely loss of your spouse might be compared with the fable of Humpty Dumpty. It can seem as if there is just no way you can put your life back together again from all the broken and scrambled pieces. However, unless you become stuck in one of the previously described tasks of grief, there will eventually come the time when you regain the opportunity to assume personal responsibility for the rest of your life. We are designed with a tremendous ability to adapt to our circumstances. Individuals have survived tumultuous catastrophes and emerged with physical and mental health. When conscious of a Higher Power, the word of life is ultimately stronger than death.

We mentioned earlier the possibility of mistaking substitution for reconstruction. This idea needs emphasizing because while it may be absolutely necessary to find or make certain substitutions for the services and presence that were provided to you by *D* _____, those substitute relationships may actually prolong your grieving process if they are confused with reconstruction.

Substitutes can fill your needs for a time but unless they become a part of your growth process of reconstruction, they may need to be abandoned as you progress through your task of rebuilding. At their best, some of the substitutes may become permanently integrated parts of your reconstructed life. At their worst, substitutes may be illusions of reconstruction that cause you double grief when you must go through the tasks of bereavement over their loss on top of your primary loss.

If your commitment to your spouse was absolute, even though you detach physically, intellectually, emotionally and spiritually, you may still need to give yourself permission to reconstruct your new life based on your own needs and wants. In fact, without such permission, reconstruction may be difficult. Grieving then can become a mode of life in itself, locking you in the tasks of Feeling and Substitution for the rest of your life. You may subconsciously limit your progress by choosing to play out the role of widow or widower as you conceive it to be, thereby closing off the opportunity for growth that is now possible.

I had set myself up for serious difficulties as I devoted my whole life outside of work to my wife and family. Whatever she wanted to do with our leisure time was my desire. During the years of her illness, I concentrated all my free time on her. After her death, I found that her friends were not my friends and that my social skills were almost totally atrophied. Oh, I could take care of the finances, keep house, meet my physical needs, and even make up my own mind about such things as which car to buy or who to support for President, but when it came to making new friends, planning social activities and tending to my emotional needs, the resources I needed were just not there. I had suppressed them for so many years that I had to begin developing them from scratch as a youth might who was just emerging from puberty. Standards of behavior had changed a great deal over the years of my withdrawal and I found myself agonizingly disoriented, as though I had come through a time warp and awakened at some future time in some strange culture. All of

my assumptions about life that had directed my behavior as a hus-
band and father seemed to be obsolete or wrong. None of my as-
sumptions seemed to fit the reality of my new condition.

Eventually you will need to consider making the transition from being widowed to being single. It may be very difficult to do and you may just have to act out the new role for a while until it becomes a natural form of new lifestyle. There is an old adage that says, *Act the way you want to be, and soon you will be the way you act.* Medical research reported by Justice and Siegel is beginning to prove this is a fact of human existence. By forcing the body to go through physical actions, the mind can be reprogrammed with a new way to think and be. Each small success reinforces your confidence to attempt more significant changes. Even though you may not feel like it for some time, if you can begin this task of reconstruction, the process may be eased along if you go through the motions anyway.

As you force yourself to take on new behavior, gradually small successes will generate positive feedback to your mind, creating additional motivation to go on to more desirable behavior. *Give yourself permission to experiment with new activities, new friends and new relationships.* Sure, you will make mistakes, but they are part of the growth process. You are a new child, adapting to a new adult world. Just forgive yourself and pick yourself up and start over again when mistakes seem to set you back. Unfortunately, you have to be your own parent to that child, giving it the care and nurture it needs to survive and grow in its new environment.

You will know that reconstruction has begun when *you can sense the future is more promising than terrifying and the past is more appreciated than a burden.* The past can exist and so can the present and it can feel good to you. Protest and despair can be replaced with hope and optimism. In a totally different way, life can become an adventure once again. This adventure can be organized into a plan that is illustrated in the following diagram. This model of life issues relates to your professional, social, personal and private relationships. To these situations, you bring resources from your whole being: physical, intellectual, emotional and spiritual.

You can use this model with the discussion to follow as a help in structuring your new life and in dealing with others in the various forms of relationships (professional, social, personal and private).

In each of these relationships we can tap the whole range of resources — physical, intellectual, emotional and spiritual — that

Table 6.1. The Lifestyle Planning Model

Resources	Professional	Social	Personal	Private
Physical				
Intellectual				
Emotional				
Spiritual				

make up our whole range of personhood. We may find ourselves in any one of the steps in this matrix at any moment in time, and we can be in more than one of them at a time. Issues in life that seem impossibly complex and totally unsolvable can be separated into their parts and dealt with in a more manageable fashion if we can sort them out, place them in this context and work on them independently. Each of us must learn to do this for ourselves, in our own way, but the following discussion may help to make this process more useful in your life at this time.

Physical Reconstruction (Step 17)

Here are some of the issues we classify as physical that may be important to your new life in the task of reconstruction:

- Food — Diet
- Medical Health — Weight Control
- Exercise — Rest — Sleep
- Housing — Clothing — Maintenance
- Transportation — Auto Operations
- Investments — Savings — Insurance
- Recreation — Vacations
- Estate — Will
- Job — Career Development
- Retirement

A whole chapter could be written on each of these issues. For a more thorough discussion of many of these topics, we recommend reading the works of Adeline McConnell and Beverly Anderson, Jane K. Burgess, and Scott Campbell and Phyllis Silverman. These authors surveyed hundreds of widowed and divorced people in mid-life and reported their creativity in managing their new situation. Their message is that life can be reconstructed but not without the impact of change, the likelihood of making mistakes and the necessity of giving yourself permission to experiment with alternatives not considered in your previous marriage relationship.

Depending upon your age and family circumstances, some of these issues will be more demanding than others. We suggest you put them in order of priority to fit your needs, from the most important to the least important. Try to set goals for yourself to accomplish, with times and dates for their completion. You may not meet all your deadlines, but having them in front of you may be a source of physical motivation, prompting you to take some action.

Setting and working toward specific physical goals can renew your interest in life. When you complete even a small task, allow yourself to feel that a little bit of reconstruction has been accomplished. In the bleak times plan only one day at a time and in the darkest moments live only one hour at a time. Try to avoid measuring your progress by anybody else's yardstick. This is progress that only you can measure, at your own pace. As the months pass, you may find that the priorities shift around, so rearrange the list to reflect your progress. Getting a list of issues down on paper can help you feel that you are doing something constructive. It will help you reduce the chaos and put some control back into your life. If you have difficulty with this task, some helpful support can be provided by a minister or rabbi, a counselor, support group or local government agencies.

Some of these issues may need to be dealt with early on if necessary physical aspects were not pre-arranged before your spouse died. Take care of the necessary physical details of life and let the others wait until you are ready.

You may have gradually and unknowingly permitted yourself to become dependent upon your spouse in many of these areas of your life. D _____'s loss may have thrown you into despair for lack of resources to manage your own life. Now you will need to learn how to reconstruct your own economic, emotional, social and intellectual activities. Gary Emery has laid out a very thorough plan for transitioning from dependence to independence. If this is your need, his work is highly recommended.

Your 10-Point Plan

Robert and Jeannette Lauer offer a 10-point plan for learning to master life's unpredictable experiences. These are:

1. *Take responsibility* for your own life but release the responsibility for significant others whom you do not control. Losses and bad luck come to all of us sooner or later; that's life. But we cannot regard ourselves as victims and continue to grow. Face the pain without artificial anesthetics; work through it, choose to grow and create a new lifestyle for yourself.
2. *Affirm your own self-worth.* Self-esteem is a precarious possession. In times of grief you can doubt your own ability, capacity and value. It is important to settle this issue if you are to grow through such a crisis.
3. *Balance concern* for yourself with concern for others. Untimely grief not only attacks our self-esteem, it can hurl us into self-absorption, harming our relationships with others. A person cannot remain totally focused on self and continue to grow.
4. *Find and use your available resources.* Some are internal and others are external. Some may have to be developed from embryonic beginnings. Assume that there are always options because there are always resources.
5. *Reframe inevitable problems* and mistakes into an adaptive, useful learning experience.
6. *Look for the positives* in otherwise undesirable situations with "silver lining" thinking. Harboring negative thinking causes a lowered sense of well-being. Positive thinking can help you to cope by enhancing your sense of well-being.
7. *Persevere but within reason.* The key is to sense when progress is being made and to move on to other alternatives when further growth is unlikely without change.
8. *Lower your threshold of awareness.* Become more sensitive to signals from others about you. Pay attention to the real world and your self-absorption will diminish, making it easier to sense new opportunities and to let go of obsolete beliefs.
9. *Restructure your life.* Use this crisis and the inevitable others to come, to redirect your character into new, appropriate changed values, beliefs and behavior.

10. *Develop personal hardiness.* Confront life and actively engage it rather than facing it passively or trying to avoid the
pain of it. Assume the degree of control over options that is
possible and engage your power to influence outcomes.
Accept change as the essence of life rather than as a threat.

The challenge, of course, is to move from knowledge of these
principles to using them in everyday life. For the devastated, grieving
survivor of a lost spouse whose lifestyle has been scrambled, this
ability may come in small, tentative steps over a long period of time.
The key for those who are successful at growing through the griefs
of life seems to be the ability to visualize yourself as the person you
want to be in the various roles you want to play with significant
others — professionally, socially, personally and privately. Such positive visual imaging is a technique used by some therapists to help
people achieve personal and professional growth. Whatever the role
being sought is, it seems that being able to "see" yourself as successfully performing in a situation is important to your probability
of achieving the goal. Conversely, if you cannot "see" yourself as
successfully performing, then the goal will be further from reality.

Intellectual Reconstruction (Step 18)

Although you may feel you are the ultimate victim in the loss of
your spouse, it is best not to maintain a victim mentality. We can
remove what Kubler-Ross has called the negativity in our lives by
consciously choosing how we will behave in response to life's experience. We might not consciously choose all that happens to us
but we can certainly choose how we respond to it. As time passes,
we can only develop in one of two directions: Either we broaden
our mental outlook, expand our knowledge and deepen our experience — or we seal ourselves up and stifle our growth behind self-
imposed intellectual walls. We participate in life or we reject it. The
alternative is to accept what is unchangeable, to change what is
possible and to know the difference. *You will finally enter reconstruction when you accept the notion that the only person in the
world who can make you happy is YOU.*

It is extremely difficult to find joy in life when you are in an
intellectual crisis. When we feel overwhelmed by change, with too
many options, too much stimulus and no reliable guidelines, there
is more confusion than joy. Now you have experienced that there are
no guarantees in life. As Nena and George O'Neill wrote, you can

never assume you are "home safe." Resignation or panic may *seem* the only alternatives, but neither is necessary.

Scott Peck likens the process of reconstruction to map-making. As we go through life, we collect a map of reality from our process of perception and decision-making, based on assumptions we make about life. Now a large portion of that map no longer accurately represents the reality of your new world. It may no longer provide dependable direction for your life. Many of your assumptions about life are no longer valid. You are in new territory. *You may need to let go of some of the basic assumptions that directed your life up to now and make a new map to follow.*

Unfortunately, this process carries a lot of risk. You must explore uncharted terrain, and you are vulnerable to failure as you attempt to construct a new lifestyle without the support of your deceased mate. Each attempt you make will be a learning experience and, eventually, you will find the way to becoming the new you that is possible.

Without risk and vulnerability there can be no growth. *Your task is to choose life and explore each possibility for growth that is now presented to you daily.* If you have struggled with the tasks to Acknowledge, Feel, Substitute and Detach, you have confronted all the forces that resist this undesired change in your life. You have plumbed the depths of your conscious and subconscious reactions, you have been immersed in darkness and you have been set on a journey that now is an ascent to freedom.

Blair Justice and Bernie Siegel have documented research results that show how physical health is related to mental health. A positive outlook on the future, a supportive social system and a feeling of being led by your Higher Power contribute to your having a satisfying future life. So you must *begin to re-explore your universe, and redraft a new map that represents the new reality of your life* more accurately. You probably don't want to but that is the task that is now set before you. You can develop a new strategy for life that will provide the flexibility to deal with the changes in your future in a positive way.

When all of our assumptions about life fail to work for us, we are naturally in a crisis. There appears to be no adequate, functional answer as we realize that we cannot retreat to what used to be. First, we sense the separation from our comfortable past set of assumptions, we experience shock and we withdraw into ourselves to conserve our emotional energy. If it appears that we have been living according to a myth all our lives, it can be a shattering experience to realize we can no longer rely on our assumptions about what is right.

Second, we may experience a change in mood and mental process as we question our perception about reality, become open to change, risk vulnerability and experiment with new behavioral options and new relationships in a period of transition.

Through the transition, we can *integrate a new set of assumptions with the old* and we can *reorganize our behavior on a new level.* It is through the new behavior that we grow. Although it is painful, such growth integrates the past with the present. In this process we get reacquainted with our inner self and we can have a new feeling of owning and directing our own lives. If we try to manage the crises of life by following old rules set down by others in accordance with the external rules of society, then stagnation and a sense of loss of self and change may bring anxiety; we can get stuck in the uncertain phase of transition, without moving on. When we learn to lead our lives in accordance with our own internal psychic needs, we can achieve ongoing growth and continuing rediscovery of self which make it possible to accept the challenges of change throughout the rest of our lives.

Every adult must experience this continuous process of change. Married couples may be able to reinforce each other during this process. Unfortunately, you no longer have that intimate relationship with D _____ or that fortress of security to bolster your process. Now we must filter out all the options for ourselves as we develop new relationships. We must assume the risk of decision-making by ourselves as we move into an unfamiliar pattern of new life. Now we must learn to manage our own lives without asking permission, without getting the approval of others, without apologizing for our mistakes, without punishing ourselves for missed opportunities, without saying "I should" or "I shouldn't," without being afraid to say "no" or "yes," and without giving up control to any other person.

The O'Neills suggest that through the transitions of life, we can seek increasing, creative maturity that will help us become more:
• Self-aware, able to be in touch with our feelings
• Centered, knowing our values and priorities
• Focused, being selective and able to make decisions
• Committed, involved with others and responsible for our actions
• Creative, innovative, flexible and open
• Autonomous, able to think for ourselves
• Compassionate, concerned, caring and understanding of others
• Competent, drawing upon all our inner physical, intellectual, emotional and spiritual resources

- Confident that we can shift with the demands of change and crisis
- Secure in the acceptance of the challenge of growth through change.

Even though times move on, change accelerates, familiar traditions and assumptions disappear and the stability of our former roots is scrambled, we can still find some peace of mind in the present if we can move through the transitional phase of crisis and on into reconstruction.

When you are ready, begin to *feed your mind new information and stimulate your senses* gradually. Once again, begin to take note of the world around you in nature and activities. Read the newspaper, subscribe to interesting magazines and observe the lives of others. If you have children, take time to learn from them. If you do not have access to your own children or grandchildren, you may be able to find some young people in your area who need your love and give them nonjudgmental attention. Getting in touch with the next generation will help you keep your mind active and your attitude in tune with the times.

Consciously *take on some new interests* gradually and set a goal to *learn some new skill* or knowledge. Some survivors go back to school. Some have to go back to work. If you are still working, begin to take on new assignments, if possible. Or seek ways to expand your job situation, make suggestions for improved productivity and show your employer that you are getting better all the time. Your intellectual growth may not require more formal education but your mind is capable of continuous learning. Don't starve it as long as it can absorb nourishment and expand.

Justice has documented research in the medical community that seems to show how the brain controls the immune system. Optimistic thoughts of better times, the feeling of being under control and having a dependable social support system are all important to the mental health of grieving people. A feeling of being connected to a Higher Power through prayer and/or meditation is also noted among successful survivors. He reported the success that writer Norman Cousins had in recovering from what is usually terminal illness by enjoying abundant laughter stimulated by old comedy movies.

Kubler-Ross emphasizes the role of music in her healing workshops. So try to *get some music and humor into your life*. You may not want to or even dislike doing so but taking in laughter and music definitely seem to be good for you in times of crisis.

Now is the time to continue to explore how thinking controls feelings. We have mentioned experts in cognitive therapy such as David Burns and Gary Emery, who have shown how changing your habits of thinking can set your life on a new course with more control of your feelings and behavior. Wayne Dyer suggests you begin by choosing to believe you have the power to control your own attitudes toward anything. Robert and Jeannette Lauer showed through many case studies that we tend to act like the kind of person we believe we are, based on life experiences that go back to our childhood. They showed how many people who suffered life-changing watershed experiences of loss and disruption actually grew in new directions as a result of changing their beliefs and thinking themselves into a new form of health.

If you hang onto the belief that you cannot help how you act and feel because that is the way your life training and experience has programmed you, then you will be stuck where you are right now. *You can resolve to control your beliefs rather than being enslaved by them.* In other words, you can choose to improve your life by changing your beliefs about yourself and your situation. However, the process may be painful and require time and investment in therapy to work out your new lifestyle.

You may have been programmed by family role models and life experiences to be dependent upon your lost spouse for many of your basic life needs. This is a time to *work on becoming more independent* in four basic aspects of your life: economic, emotional, social and intellectual.

This is a time to consciously and deliberately *evaluate your personal relationships* with family members, friends and co-workers. You can become aware of your ego boundaries, the conscious awareness of self. Each of us maintains an ego space or boundary that protects us from being victimized by unscrupulous, manipulating others. You can become susceptible to control by others when your ego boundaries are down but tightly shutting off your ego boundaries forecloses the nurturing support that might be available from caring others. A balance is needed.

Select new friends carefully. Break down the old barriers to change and permit yourself to make overtures to people instead of waiting for someone to invite you into their life. Reach out to new people who appeal to you. *Let go of both new and old relationships that are not supportive,* even though it will be painful to admit those relationships no longer are a part of your life. Grieve for their loss and let go, give them up and go on. Have the courage to walk away from situations in which the potential burdens outweigh the potential benefits before you make an irrevocable physical, intellectual, emotional or spiritual investment in them.

Do the kinds of things you like to do and go to the places where you like to go. Until you begin to detach from *D* _____ you may not want to do anything at all, especially if you were dependent upon your spouse for your social life. Apathy may sap away your interest in life and dull your senses so no pain or pleasure can affect you during the feeling task of grief. Later you can begin to tentatively experiment a little with activities you never had the time or money to do until now. It may take extra energy and assumption of risk to begin making new contacts and getting involved in a new social circle but without risk there is no opportunity.

As you gain confidence and renew your self-esteem, your self-image will improve. Ever so gradually you will once again be an enjoyable person to socialize with. Different, but neat. Seek intellectual balance in your life. Reduce the tendency to evaluate, assess, analyze and interpret the world and practice enjoying, being and doing. Just learning to participate in life without cursing reality all the time, and thereby blocking any chance for happiness in the now, can be a first step in your reconstruction.

As you develop a wider social circle, you may find others seeking new friends also. It isn't easy and it is risky to offer yourself to others because you are vulnerable to rejection. As any good salesman knows, it may take several rejections to find one acceptance so look at rejections as necessary steps on the way to acceptance. Don't take them personally. You can either let fear of rejection prevent you from developing a new life or you can plow through your fears and take on the challenge of growth. Yes, you may be afraid to venture out and make the social scene again on your own this time. Unfortunately, some people in this society are insensitive and if you exhibit signs of distress and disability, there are those who will reject you. That, in turn, will continually refuel your grief and destroy your self-esteem. So screw up your courage and put your mind to work for you while you fight off its attempts to work against you.

The best cure for painful old memories is to create a series of pleasant new memories that intervene to help stifle the suffering caused by the old ones. Use your thinking to *plan stimulating activities and invite people into your life who will help you build a new set of healing memories.* This is especially important around holidays and other commemorative days such as anniversaries and birthdays.

Do not permit yourself to be alone on such days, if at all possible. Create new traditions to replace the obsolete ones. If you must be alone at such times, try to be alone with others in some form of public, group activities. Do everything possible to stimulate your intellectual powers at such times.

If decision-making is a problem for you, here is a step-by-step procedure to help you evaluate any set of options, giving you more confidence and reducing the element of risk involved. For each problem you must solve, describe or list the several options under consideration on separate sheets of paper. Divide each sheet into two columns, one for benefits or advantages and one for burdens or disadvantages. List as many of each as you think of for each option. Then give each benefit or burden a weight from 1 to 100, depending on your own values and understanding of their importance to you. In setting the weights, let your intuition and feelings enter into the decision along with your logic and thinking. Add up the weights for each group, and give the benefits a positive number and the burdens a negative number. Sum the two and enter a final total weight for each of your options. Then, when all options are completed, look for the one with the highest positive score. That may be your best choice, given what you know and how you value the options.

Emotional Reconstruction (Step 19)

The search for new balance in your life will include redirecting your emotions away from grief and toward reconstruction. In addition to rebuilding your self-esteem, you may have to confront and reconstruct your beliefs about the two basic emotions, fear and love. The only way to avoid future grief is to avoid love. In order to experience love, you must engage in relationships with other people and that is a fearsome prospect for many who must adjust to single living after many years of happy marriage. Managing that fear may require that you rethink your basic beliefs about love and self-esteem.

Some fears are learned reactions to any unfamiliar territory or activity. Other fears come from involuntary, subconscious reactions of different sections of the brain. At its basic level, what we fear most may be the realization of our own mortality and the certainty of our own death. Whatever their source, fears can prevent you from moving ahead in your life or stimulate you to action in your own defense. You need to decide which of these responses to fear you will let rule your life.

According to Susan Jeffers, in order to move ahead you need to *learn how to convert fear into power, struggle into adventure, problems into opportunities and hope into confidence.* The four basic truths about fear described by Jeffers apply very well to reconstructing your emotional life in grief.

The first basic truth is that fear will never go away so long as you are growing. It only leaves you at the moment of death. The second truth is that the only way to get rid of the fear of doing something is to do it. Truth number three is that pushing yourself through fear is less damaging than living with it. The fourth truth is that love and the power to overcome fear go together. Her thesis is that we choose to live the way we do because we all have power to change our lives if we want to. You may not feel such power in your life for a long time but eventually the opportunity will begin to emerge if you seek genuine love as the antidote to fear.

Howard Halpern suggested that the greatest devastation a person can suffer is when he has placed all his needs for closeness, connection, nurturance and identity in one person and then loses that person. In his state of bitter grief, he may vow never again to join in an intimate, emotional relationship with another. As you conquer fear and begin to overcome the anxiety, guilt and jealousy, you can become more open to love and possibly marriage once again. Or, in your new strength, you may decide that being single has its advantages and is the way you wish to spend the rest of your life.

The role of love in our lives is seen differently by different authors. David Viscott and Abraham Maslow think love is a valid need of the human being. David Burns wrote that love is not a necessary factor in achieving mental health or happiness. He proposed that seeking after love when it is not available is only contributing to depression. Stanton Peele claims romantic love is an ideal vehicle for addiction because it can so exclusively claim a person's consciousness, separating us from a full life as we concentrate on the isolated satisfaction of the next "fix" of being with the object of our physical affection. We have already seen how traumatic separation can be for those who depend so much on another.

I felt like a baby separated from its mother. I seemed to be running around with my umbilical cord in my hand, looking for another person to plug into for my continued survival. This feeling of need is still a part of me and likely will be for the rest of my life but I am learning to be aware of the infantile sources of this need and to channel it for my own good. Paradoxically, the more I tried to control life, the more I seemed to lose control of it. I learned through anxiety and panic, oh so gradually and feebly, that letting go and trusting in the spiritual essence of my being was the best way of meeting my emotional problems. But my ego still wants to be in charge.

This concept, offering love as a solution to fear, is the theme of the work of Gerald Jampolsky, based on the concepts in *A Course in Miracles* and other such philosophies. The basic message is in the following compilation of Jampolsky's 12 principles of attitudinal healing from *Love Is Letting Go Of Fear:*

> The essence of our being is love. Health is inner peace. Healing is letting go of fear. Giving and receiving are the same. We can let go of the past and the future. Now is the only time there is and each instant is for giving. We can learn to love ourselves and others by forgiving rather than judging. We can become love finders rather than fault finders. We can choose and direct ourselves to be peaceful inside regardless of what is happening outside. We are students and teachers to each other. We can focus on the whole of life rather than the fragments. Since love is eternal, death need not be viewed as fearful. We can always perceive others as either extending love or giving a call for help.

To paraphrase Susan Jeffers, *"feel the fear, and do it anyway"* — *with love.*

Another contemporary view of mature love was described by Peck. He emphasizes that genuine love is not cathexis, it is not dependency, it is not self-sacrifice and it is not the erotic ecstasy or feelings associated with passion. On the other hand, love is the work of attention, of listening to the needs of the other. It contains the risk of rejection or loss. It is the process of growing up to independence. It is the act of commitment through the issues of life. It is risk of confrontation born of humility. Love is the disciplined exercise of fidelity and freedom and love is the separateness of individuals with their own destinies to fulfill. As reported by Jampolsky, Kubler-Ross, Justice and Siegel, unconditional, nonjudgmental love is also the source of much healing for many people who learn to live in relationships with others in this mode.

When love develops out of friendship, it is likely to be more enduring. The process of friendship should not be rushed or confused with the task of substitution, as discussed before. It takes time for friendship to mature into genuine love. All new acquaintances do not develop into friends. Give yourself permission to experiment and make mistakes in your new relationships.

You may need to decide whether to concentrate most of your attention on one exclusive loving relationship at a time or divide it among several less intense friendships. Some counselors suggest *you need platonic friendships at various levels of intimacy.* It's important to remember that it takes time, commitment and energy to maintain a truly intimate friendship or love relationship. One of the miracles of genuine love, however, is that it expands to meet the opportunity. As more opportunities for loving are presented to you, your ability to take advantage of them will grow. As you permit the growth of love in your life, your emotional life will have less and less room for despair, depression, sadness or self-pity. Of course, you may decide to keep your ego boundary tightly closed and not allow anyone to ever get that close.

Although experts do not agree about what is essential in life, they do agree that we all need an adequate sense of self-esteem. It is especially important to bereaved spouses who may acutely miss the self-esteem provided by the acceptance and approval of the one they lost. When life does not treat us as we think it should or as we assume we deserve, we may conclude that we are worthless. The resulting pain can drive us into unhealthy ways of behaving or relating. People in this state of mind can do harm to themselves through alcohol or drug abuse, promiscuous sex, overeating or other types of compulsive indulgence. Learning something about modern concepts regarding self-esteem can help you avoid such unfortunate reactions.

The "self" is thought by Louis Gottschalk to actually consist of four components:

1. *The ideal, perfectly endowed self* of our subconscious
2. *The reflected self* that we obtain through the mirror reflection or response from significant others in our lives
3. *The negative self* or the one we are not very proud of
4. *The real world self* that evolves from our character and personality, the one that makes up our internal focus of existence.

If your spouse provided the reflected self that you came to depend upon for your self-esteem, the real self may not be well developed and must be reconstructed through new activities and relationships.

Gradually through therapy I became aware of the dependency I had upon D Rosalene for my self-esteem and my identity. Without her or some female substitute to accept me sexually as a man, I

*actually felt dead inside. I doubted that I could ever live alone or
be at peace, comfortable with my own company. I seemed to exist
only through the reflected acceptance provided by D Rosalene.
Without her or someone else in my life, I was threatening to destroy
my physical self and my intellectual self because my emotional self
was so deprived of this reflected image. I had to begin developing
a whole new basis for my self-esteem. It was neither easy nor quick
and it is still a continuing process.*

If we do not have a well-constructed real self from childhood
development (and few of us do because our parents were not
perfect either), reconstruction of the reflected self must come from
having the acceptance and reinforcement of significant others in our
lives. We are social creatures and we can wither and die if we are
forced into a life of isolation. According to Gary Smalley and John
Trent, this need for acceptance is met by meaningful touch, by
verbal affirmation through a spoken message of approval, by a
feeling of high value of self, by picturing a successful future, and by
active commitment on the part of loved ones that gives us intimate
social involvement. If this need is not met during our first three
years of life, we can be hungry for it the rest of our lives.

Self-esteem can also be improved by doing something compe-
tently which you value so the completion of it will give you a
sense of accomplishment to boost your worth and self-image. If
we lacked sufficient nurturing through this form of "blessing"
from our childhood, we must learn to reconstruct our lives to
obtain it for ourselves and provide it to those meaningful others
with whom we live out the rest of our days. Those widowed
people who are not part of an integrated family structure may find
a sense of belonging in support groups or other social groups,
such as churches or clubs and be able to share in the sense of self-
worth that results.

Now may be the time to begin reaching out to others in need of
what you have to give. In fact, it may be that *by providing nurturing self-esteem for others, self-esteem is somehow increased in
ourselves.* Jesus spoke of this reverse phenomenon when he said,
"Give and it will be given to you; good measure, pressed down,
shaken together, running over, will be put into your lap. For the
measure you give will be the measure you get back" (Luke 6:38).
In our experience, giving almost always seems to lead to receiving
even more than was given.

You may feel pretty awkward, maybe even embarrassed, the first few times you try to initiate new social contacts. It can be a draining experience for certain introverted personality types. Depending upon the strength of your needs, you may or may not find the potential results worth the effort. Some people find this need partly met in family relations. Others may find it met temporarily in relations with a special friend or professional counselor who can play the reinforcing role for you. For others, it can come through contact with church or fraternal groups. For those still actively working, it may be sought in a drive for professional job enlargement. Chances are you will need to modify this need as you move farther away from your detachment to *D* _____.

You may need to reconfirm a sense of your own self-worth outside of these socially derived sources. According to Burns, true self-esteem may be found only in the realization that you are as worthy as everybody else, regardless of your material possessions or professional status, personal recognition, social accomplishments or their lack, in comparison with others. You may need to relearn how to measure your self-worth by your own yardstick and that of no one else. In the process of seeking self-esteem, you must guard against being victimized by those who purposefully or unknowingly tend to use your needy emotional condition to meet their own needs, without contributing significantly to yours.

Humans can be very predatory when it comes to the weaker members of society. As Wayne Dyer described the situation, we must guard against being manipulated and learn to master our own lives or, as he says, "pull your own strings." The balance between protecting yourself from victimization and learning to give unconditional, nonjudgmental love poses a challenge that demands great courage. For people in grief this can be an extremely energy-consuming process, one that may benefit from professional counseling.

The fact is that a number of widows and widowers will remain single in their new life. Being alone, by itself, is neither painful nor joyous. As Thomas Wolfe has suggested, it is our thoughts about being alone that create our feelings about it. If you are going to live alone, keep in mind what Anthony Storr said — that in solitude we can cope with the stress of loss, learn self-reliance and engage in self-discovery. Storr's examination of the healing value of solitude during periods of mourning and stress, the creative solitude of sleep and the strong relationship between solitude, creativity and spiritual awareness, offer new insight into the essential role of solitude for thinking, imaginative people.

How To Overcome Loneliness

For those for whom being alone is not an opportunity but a heavy burden, John Hritzuk and others suggest the following plan to overcome loneliness:

1. Compile a list of everyone you know including friends, acquaintances, relatives, etc. Try to include some things you know they are interested in. If this list is too short for comfort, work on getting more new people into your life.
2. Contact at least one friend each day to discuss what you are doing and what interests them.
3. Identify your interests and get involved in activities that act on them. You never meet anybody new if you stay at home alone. (If you were socially dependent upon your spouse, this can be an energy-consuming task.)
4. Try to find substitutes for the missing contribution that was made to your life by your deceased spouse. Pinpoint what you are missing the most and make the effort to fill that void.
5. Try to balance your time by adjusting your schedule to make room for visiting or phoning people who can make you feel better.
6. Separate friends from acquaintances and concentrate on building true friendships, even if only with two or three good friends with whom you have the most in common.
7. Acknowledge loneliness as part of your life and indulge yourself in solitary treats or gifts that contribute to your self-esteem and are a reward for tolerating your condition.
8. Get a pet because it can give you unconditional love when human love is absent.
9. Learn what your needs really are and avoid people and situations that do not contribute to them and that compound your loneliness. Look for activities that make you feel good about yourself.
10. Care for your body with sufficient rest, exercise and diet to minimize risk of health problems. You don't need any such complications in addition to your emotional situation.

Obviously, this list of things to do is much easier to write than it is to carry out. As Peck reminds us, life is struggle and life is solving problems. If we can accept that fact of life, then its joys may be more evident. We can even learn to develop new traditions in single life to replace the traditions of our former coupled life.

Spirituality And Reconstruction (Step 20)

Like the other steps of grief, those of spiritual growth in your reconstruction can be taken only by you. There are no instruction books for you to use, either. Nevertheless, we think those who search can be hopeful about finding.

Halpern has pointed out how unrealistic it is to deny the transient nature of every human relationship. He believes that the more we root our attachment needs to things more lasting and timeless, the firmer we can stand during life's changes and endings. Some people find strength, awe and a feeling of being part of the universe when they observe the splendors of natural wonders, such as are found in our national parks. Others are more oriented toward the animate, feel connected with all living things and have a sense of kinship with all of humankind. For many, the "lasting and timeless" is found in communing with a Supreme Being or Higher Power or however they understand God, either through formal religious doctrine and ritual or through another form of worship.

When someone who has lost a loved spouse is able to feel, "I am not alone because I know God loves me," or "I am part of a greater universal plan," he or she may experience a feeling of belonging that fulfills these basic human attachment needs and may feel less alone. You can make the effort to become more open to a wide range of spiritual expressions and experiences that will expand your boundaries of consciousness with new potential sources for satisfying your spiritual needs.

Those who identify in themselves a spiritual core are more likely to experience a sense of spiritual connectedness with other people, society, the world, the chain of life and the cosmos. A mature concept of your infinite connectedness with the universe, which includes an awareness of your brief time in human history in the context of infinite space, may help free you during this time of Reconstruction. *The opportunity of Reconstruction, from a spiritual perspective, is the opportunity of a new life in which there are blessings waiting for you.* You are free to reject your future but if you keep working at your spiritual development, the growth and blessing waiting for you will begin to unfold.

We know how hard it is to find spiritual comfort when you are suffering grief. We realize that for various personality types growth in spirituality follows different paths. Those who share a spiritual sensitivity also know that somehow or other we are all interrelated in a grander design. From this awareness, healing can come.

As I review this section, it is spring again. The early flowers are out, the grass is turning green and beginning to grow, the leaves are bursting through the brown buds and the birds have come back from their southern winter vacations. These are sensory perceptions related to the physical world of resurrection. There is a deeper, intuitive feeling about this time of year.

In my deepest grief, I did not care what day it was, what hour it was or what season it was. Now, after nearly five years, I am beginning to look about me to see the beautiful earth once again. And I am beginning to rediscover my connection to it. I am also able to recall how my beloved <u>D Rosalene</u> responded to the coming of spring each year. I recall how she got out her lighter, more colorful clothing and how she began to open up the house to the warming light of the sun. I recall how she wanted to get out into the air and how she began to give me instructions about what she wanted done about the house. I recall how we worked together on spring cleaning projects, washing away the grime of winter, painting and renewing our space once again. I recall the plans for weekend camping that we enjoyed in those years and I recall with joy how we looked forward to the weekend excursions and plans for summer vacation.

Now, it is up to me to make those plans for myself, with only my Higher Power to guide me. So it is for you also. I step forward in faith.

Faith is trust that God is an ever-present source of love and support. Faith does not require proof or evidence. It is a confidence and a reliance not on the power of the intellect to know, but on the One who created the intellect with all its strengths and limitations. Saul of Tarsus, a Jewish leader who became the Apostle Paul, wrote: "So we do not lose heart. Though our outer nature is wasting away, our inner nature is being renewed every day. For this slight momentary affliction is preparing for us an eternal weight of glory beyond all comparison, because we look not to the things that are seen but to the things that are unseen; for the things that are seen are transient, but the things that are unseen are eternal" (II Corinthians 4:16-18).

Oh yes, I still feel outraged and wronged by God and disappointed that some of those I expected to care let me down, just as I have unresolved grievances against my parents and <u>D Rosalene</u>. But I cannot stop loving my family nor can I stop loving God, my creator, even though I have been wounded by grief. God and I have been

*through a traumatic experience together and the final outcome is
still not certain. I know that whatever comes, I am not alone.*

Those who pray usually think of prayer as a way to communicate with God, however they understand God. The flow of communication is understood to go both ways but most who pray use
it as an occasion to speak more than as a time to listen. In spite of
our determination to run our own lives, there may be wisdom in
opening yourself to trying to understand what higher purpose
your life may serve, now that you are single again and at the point
of reconstructing your life. Such a stance might be expressed in a
***request for God's guidance, an open mind to receive it, and the
courage to act on it.***

For those for whom prayer is a foreign experience or one you find
no longer helpful, ***meditation may serve both as a calming method
and a way to get in touch with a Higher Power.*** Scientific research
from all over the world has indicated there is a reserve or core of
consciousness buried deep within the mind that can be tapped for
renewed energy and peace of mind. Meditation is listening to this
still small voice within. It is a way of opening our conscious minds
to the power of the subconscious spiritual resources. Some believe it
is a method of accessing the imaginative creativity located in the
right side of the human brain. Developing a routine, regular and
sustained form of meditation is a very useful therapy for reconstruction. It is one of the channels through which our spiritual energy can
be put to active, practical use. It is a means for approaching daily life
with more love, joy, peace, patience, kindness, goodness, faithfulness,
gentleness and self-control (Galatians 5:22-23).

One other aspect in spiritual renewal is worth mentioning. There
are not many "God is" sentences in the Bible. One of them is "God
is light." This statement has a specific meaning in Scripture that has
to be understood in the appropriate context. However, if you just let
your mind associate for a moment with the idea of *light,* there are
several ways you might let that light shine on your task of Reconstruction. Science tells us that light is a form of electromagnetic
energy and that color is a perceived segment of the overall band of
detectable energy. Color, then, derives from light. The latest findings
in the science of color perceptions indicate that people can find a
higher level of peace and serenity in an environment where the
colors are compatible with their personal tastes. Reconstruction
might be the time to ***take a look around you to see whether the
colors in your living environment and wardrobe adequately***

reflect "you." Those who have asked this question and made the appropriate changes usually report that the changes were helpful.

Since daylight is a pure form of all color combinations, taking in daylight as a regular daily routine is also known to be helpful in alleviating depression and providing renewal. Experiencing a full measure of light can be a delightful diet for your spiritual recon-struction. *Open the curtains or blinds in your house and let the sunshine into your life.*

Another way to let God's light into your life is to give yourself in loving service to others. Medical science is beginning to uncover mysteries about functions in the brain that seem to prove that when we give unconditional love through service to others, we indeed do stimulate our own internal forces for healing. So as soon as you are strong enough, and maybe even before, *find someone who needs what you have to give (even if it is only a little of your time). Give it to them in a nonjudgmental, loving way,* and you will take another step toward Reconstruction.

Give yourself permission to be patient. You are going through the temper of fire in your process of reconstruction from grief. And as the blacksmith heats the metal to softness in order to reshape it into a useful product, so you are shaping yourself into a new person. It is painful and it takes time to overcome your involuntary separation from *D* _____. The results to be obtained from this task of reconstruction may take longer than you like. The pace of contempory life too often teaches us to expect instant solutions to our problems. Now you are being taught patience and the learn-ing is hard. It will take the rest of your life for you to grow into the new person that you are becoming.

We have now completed a brief discussion of the 20 Steps covered in our new model of grief work. We hope that you have found our model to be of help to you. Undoubtedly, you found some sections of this discussion to be more meaningful or useful than others. We suggest that may be related to your personality preferences and characteristics. Different personalities seem to identify with some parts of the model more than they do with others. In the chapter to follow, we will talk about the different kinds of personality types and how an understanding of your own personality can be of help in your recovery from loss and your growth through grief. Then we will relate this model of grief work more specifically to the problems of survivors in dysfunctional families.

7

Personalities And Grief

The ways in which people grieve vary from person to person and from situation to situation. For some people the grief process is painful but relatively uncomplicated. For others, the process can become pathological, leading to physical and/or emotional illness. There is a gray area in which reactions to grief can be very severe and yet not call for medical or psychological treatment. The Diagnostic and Statistical Manual III of the American Psychiatric Association does not classify normal grief as a mental illness, although it may look and feel like a serious problem to the person who is caught in its severest phases. It is possible, however, to distinguish normal from pathological grief.

In the 1940s, Erich Lindemann described several symptoms of distorted grief reactions. Among these are marked overactivity without a sense of loss; physical symptoms belonging to the terminal illness of the deceased; certain psychosomatic disorders including ulcerative colitis and asthma; a withdrawal from relationships with friends and relatives; overflowing hostility spread out over all relationships; absence of emotional display resulting in a masklike appearance with formal, stilted, robotlike movements; restlessness coupled with lack of motivation for any type of activities shared with others; a hypergenerosity including foolish financial dealings and self-punitive giving away of valuable family possessions; and, finally, agitated depression, insomnia, feelings of worthlessness and bitter self-accusation with needs for self-punishment that could lead to suicide.

The revised Diagnostic and Statistical Manual of the American Psychiatric Association (DSM-III-R) includes such symptoms as "morbid preoccupation" with feelings of worthlessness, prolonged difficulty in doing the things the person normally has done and marked slowing down of the ability to think, feel and act.

In normal grief a survivor usually moves fairly consistently along in the process, with some periodic setbacks, of course. If any of the challenges that grief presents appear insurmountable, if the survivor gets stuck in one task or cannot seem to complete it and move on, if the process is extended beyond a year or so, or if the intensity of suffering is so great as to cause the kind of behavior dysfunction we described above, then we recommend immediate professional consultation and treatment.

What is appropriate grief for your particular situation is difficult to say, so a professional perspective can be very helpful. Grief reactions range from relatively mild to very severe. It all depends upon the relationship, the overall circumstances of the loss, how you are equipped to deal with the demands the loss imposes and what physical, intellectual, emotional and spiritual resources are available to aid you in the necessary reconstruction.

Another variable that may be very important in how a person responds to grief is that individual's unique personality. Although more research is needed on applications of the 20-step model, co-author Dr. Gary Harbaugh's research and writing show a connection between personality types and the experience of loss. We believe that if those who experience loss understand their own personality traits, preferences and characteristics they will be better able to deal with their grief and recover more fully from their loss.

In this chapter we are going to take a close look at how persons with different types of personalities are likely to experience the process of grief. To do this, we shall overlay the 20-step model of grief work that we introduced earlier with a description of the personality types identified by the Myers-Briggs Type Indicator (MBTI).

The Myers-Briggs Type Indicator®

First, let's review and expand our earlier description of the personality characteristics described by the MBTI:

Table 7.1. MBTI Model Of Personality

(E) Extraversion _____ | _____ Introversion (I)	
Outer or Inner World/Source of Energy	
(S) Sensing _____ | _____ Intuition (N)	
Perception: Way of Taking in Information	
(T) Thinking _____ | _____ Feeling (F)	
Judgment: Decision-Making	
(J) Judgment _____ | _____ Perception (P)	
What Outside World Sees: Lifestyle	

Recall from the previous explanation that this model results in the classification of people into 16 different personality types. For example, a person may be an Extraverted, Sensing, Thinking, Judging type (resulting in a four letter designation: ESTJ) who prefers the choices on the left side of the scale above. Or a person may be an Extraverted, Sensing, Thinking, Perceptive type (ESTP) who prefers three from the left and one on the right. Or someone may be any of the possible combinations that result in the 16 different personality types. In the four-letter description, i.e., ISTJ, ENFP, etc., note that *N* is used for Intuition, as *I* is used for Introversion. Therefore, an INTP personality has a personality preference for Introversion, Intuition, Thinking and Perception.

According to the MBTI (which, remember, is based on the psychological theory of Carl Gustav Jung), each person has a unique personality that arises out of the interaction of that person's preferences for one or another side of each of the four polarities. While the polarities are represented by the four scales: Extraversion-Introversion, Sensing-Intuition, Thinking-Feeling, Judgment-Perception, even the extroverted person uses introversion sometimes and vice-versa. No one is completely one-sided on any of the above four scales but each person seems to have a preference for one over its opposite (Extraversion *or* Introversion, Sensing *or* Intuition, etc.). The personality preferences we have are usually the ones we develop more fully. We could, therefore, expect that a person who prefers Extraversion will typically develop that preference and be more comfortable in situations which call for extraversion.

As noted before, the Myers-Briggs Type Indicator (MBTI) is a psychological instrument designed to help identify which Jungian type you prefer. It identifies the direction and clarity of preference on each of the four scales. The MBTI was developed on the basis of more than 20 years of case by case study, followed by years of research.

In 1975, Consulting Psychologists Press (CPP) became the publisher and the MBTI is now reported to be among the fastest-growing psychological instruments in the country. It has gained widespread popularity among professional counselors in fields such as counseling (careers, relationship counseling, etc.), religion, organizational development and management, education, etc. The Center for Applications of Psychological Type (CAPT) conducts research and provides education and training for those who want to learn more about specific applications of the MBTI. To promote the professional and ethical use of the MBTI, the Association for Psychological Type (APT) was formed. Both CAPT and APT are headquartered in Gainesville, Florida (their addresses are in Gary's *Afterword*). Through APT, you can learn about their training programs designed to prepare professionals to meet CPP's qualifications to administer the MBTI and interpret the results. We believe that if you know your personality type, you will have a valuable tool for understanding your reactions to loss and managing untimely grief.

How can differences in personality affect the way a person responds to loss? In order to apply the MBTI to our 20-step model of grief, we need to take you a little further along in your understanding of what the MBTI actually indicates. The description that follows is paraphrased with permission from an inexpensive and very useful booklet, **Introduction to Type,** a publication of Consulting Psychologists Press, 577 College Avenue, Palo Alto, CA 94306.

Personality Function Dynamics

In order to deal with any situation in life, people need both what the MBTI calls "Perception" and "Judgment." Perception is a way of "seeing," a way of taking in information. Then judgment is needed, which means a person needs a way of deciding which of the available options is most appropriate or desirable. Through the unique combination of these "functions" of personality, each person exhibits his or her personal behavior.

Perception is of two types, either *Sensing* or *Intuition* (S or N). People who prefer Sensing perception use their senses (eyes, ears, etc.) for gathering the specific facts about the situation or people. The Sensing person usually pays very close attention to these facts. People who prefer Intuitive perception see not so much the particulars as the patterns, relationships and possibilities that are beyond the physical senses. They move rather quickly into what the facts mean and how they are related.

The *Intuitive* person is not as present-oriented as the Sensing person. Intuitive people are more future-oriented, looking for possibilities that include but go beyond the physical senses. Most people use both sensing and intuition but not at the same time and not usually with equal confidence. You are likely to use the one you prefer more and therefore become more skilled at using it. Sensing people tend to be observant and to become realistic, practical and good at remembering facts and working with them. People who prefer intuition tend to value imagination and inspiration and are interested in new ideas, projects and abstract problem-solving.

Perhaps you can already see some ways in which the way we perceive may affect how we respond to a loss situation. Before we explore these connections further, let's be sure we understand what the MBTI means by *Judgment*. Everyone has to have both a way of perceiving and a way of judging. There are two kinds of judgment, according to Jung, Thinking and Feeling. Each of these types of Judgment is a rational process (yes, Feeling judgment is a *rational* process as explained by Jung, not to be confused with emotionality).

In decision-making, *Thinking* people prefer to decide analytically, on the basis of logical cause and effect. The rationale that Feeling types use in making decisions is different. People who prefer feeling judgment are more likely to take into account personal values and feelings important both to themselves and the other people involved in the decision, without requiring that the decision be logical. The Thinking decision is therefore more objective, the Feeling decision more personal value centered. The Thinking person strives for a just and fair decision. A rational decision for a Feeling person is based on people's feelings and is intended to maintain or restore harmonious interpersonal relationships.

If you trust and use Thinking more, you tend to become most skillful in dealing with people and events when they follow a logical order. If you trust Feeling more, you tend to become better at dealing with people through the use of sympathy, tact, etc. Feeling people therefore may be seen more sensitive to the feelings of others, as well as their own.

The kind of perception you prefer can be combined with either kind of judgment, so there are four possible combinations of these functions of personality: Sensing plus Thinking (ST), Sensing plus Feeling (SF), Intuition plus Feeling (NF) and Intuition plus Thinking (NT). A brief comparison of ST, SF, NF and NT is shown in the following table (reprinted with permission of Consulting Psychologists Press).

Table 7.2. Summary Of Personality Functions

People who prefer:	ST	SF	NF	NT
Focus their attention on:	Realities	Realities	Possibilities	Possibilities
and handle these with:	Objective Analysis	Personal Warmth	Personal Warmth	Objective Analysis
Thus they tend to become:	Practical and analytical	Sympathetic and friendly	Enthusiastic and insightful	Logical and analytical
and find scope for their abilities in:	Technical skills with objects and facts	Practical help and services for people	Understanding and communicating with people	Theoretical and technical developments

Does one of the columns seem to describe you better? Taking the MBTI will help you identify which is more truly you. People can do many, perhaps all, of these things, but only one of these combinations is your "best fit" psychological type or "personality gift." People opposite to you are likely to be weaker where you are stronger and stronger where you are weaker. Each type has its own set of strengths and abilities — and its limitations.

In a tough situation, a really good decision requires us to use all the personality gifts (even though only two of them are more natural to us). For example, you should use your Sensing for paying attention to facts and being realistic. Use your Intuition to discover all the possibilities, not just the ones you first observe. Use your Thinking to evaluate all the options, both pleasant and unpleasant, trying to count the cost of everything and examining every misgiving without letting personal loyalties interfere with this objective analysis. Use your Feeling to weigh how deeply you care about the alternatives (which are closest to your primary values), to consider how other people will respond and finally to decide on a solution that will work out for the best.

You can see how ignoring any of these functions can possibly lead to trouble in decision-making but you will probably rely primarily on a decision-making process that appeals to your dominant personality gifts. Intuitives may base a decision on some possibility without paying much attention to facts that might be crucial if the possibility they see is ever to come about. Sensing persons may settle for a single solution because they do not naturally look for all the other possibilities. Thinking types may overlook human concerns and values. Feeling types may ignore the logical, long-range consequences of a given decision, no matter how people-pleasing it appears to be at first glance. It is amazing how different a situation can look to two people of opposite types.

The E-I scale on the Myers-Briggs Type Indicator describes where you like to use your most preferred (Dominant) function. For example, Extraverts prefer to use their dominant personality gift in the outside world of things and people. Introverts prefer to use their dominant gift in their inner world. Extraverts tend to become energized working with people and things while Introverts tend to be energized by activities that take place inside — reflecting on facts, ideas, concepts, theories, etc.

The scale on the bottom (J-P) identifies which personality preference the outside world is most likely to see (whether it is your dominant personality gift or not). If a person has an MBTI type that ends with a J, that means the outside world probably sees their way of judging or deciding. In our society, some people may be uncomfortable being identified as a Judging type. They may think that the MBTI Judging type means they are judgmental. That is not what the MBTI means by a Judging type. Actually, the J stands for a person who faces the world in a planned, orderly way, wanting to regulate and control life. The world is likely to see their T (Thinking) or their F (Feeling), whichever of the two they prefer. A J person also prefers to get necessary decisions made and, if they are also extraverted (EJ), usually come to conclusions quickly.

Perceptive types prefer to rely on their preferred Sensing or Intuition in dealing with the outer world and tend to live in a flexible, spontaneous way, wanting to understand life and adapt to it. Perceptives tend to put off making decisions not because they procrastinate but because they prefer to take in all the alternatives and not come to closure prematurely. In decision-making, the J person therefore has to be on guard so as not to come to a conclusion a little too quickly. The P person needs to be sure the decision is reached quickly enough.

Remember that by definition the Extraverts use their dominant (probably also their favorite) function in dealing with the outer world while Introverts keep their dominant function to themselves and usually use their auxiliary or second function in the outer world. Thus with the Extravert, what you see may well be their "best." What you see with Introverts, is usually only their second best. They keep their preferred and typically most developed function inside and usually share it openly with people they feel comfortable with.

If there are most-preferred personality functions, that means there are also least-preferred functions. Jung related these to the less conscious side of personality. If Thinking judgment is our favorite (Dominant) personality trait, then the exact opposite of the Dominant is the Inferior or least preferred function. Jung also wrote about the Shadow and some people confuse the Inferior with the Shadow but the two are different. Our Inferior (or least-preferred) function may be the source of some of our reaction to stress but it is also thought to contribute to our creativity and personal renewal. The one remaining personality function is called the tertiary or third function. It is possible to rank the four functions in terms of the Dominant, Auxiliary, Tertiary and Inferior.

This ranking designates the personality functions in terms of their likely order of preference, and the ranking may also be an indication of their *probable* degree of development. Both order of preference and degree of development are related to how a person might best manage grief, as we shall see.

Jung thought it is possible for us to become more aware of the undeveloped sides of our personality as we get older. In mid-life and later, a mature and growing person seems to be naturally motivated to improve their use of the less-preferred personality characteristics. This could be an instinctive drive to become a more integrated person. This tendency toward integration is unlikely to begin prior to mid-life.

I became aware of how significant the loss of D Rosalene was in my life when I realized that her ENFP type was a perfect complement to my ISTJ. We were opposites on all four scales. This meant we had very different ways of perceiving and deciding on life issues. In our case, we learned how to adapt and team up for the best use of our individual strengths. I did not have to develop the opposite side of my personality — I had it in her!

With her loss, the devastating feeling of deprivation and amputation might be explained by this aspect of our relationship. Now it became more important than ever that I work on developing the missing sides of my own personality in order to compensate for her loss. Spouses whose preferences are more similar might not be able to identify exactly with the kind of loss I felt because of the way I had relied on my wife's strengths.

With this background, it is now possible to display the characteristics frequently associated with the 16 possible personality type combinations in a table based on **Introduction to Type** (again, with the kind permission of Consulting Psychologists Press, Inc.). To assist our later discussion the Dominant (most preferred) function is underlined for each type.

Everyone possesses some of the characteristics of personality types other than their own, but a person will usually exhibit personality preferences that primarily effect one of the 16 types. *Without taking the MBTI, you should not come to a definite conclusion about which personality type is most accurate for you.* You may have found certain words or phrases in several of the types describing a characteristic you sometimes show or a skill you sometimes employ. Since we use all the preferences at one time or another, this is to be expected. With proper administration and interpretation of the MBTI, most people are able to identify the type that is more truly their particular combination of personality gifts.

The MBTI And Reactions To Loss Situations

Now let's see how personality may affect the way a person responds to grief. To apply the MBTI to the 20 steps model of

Characteristics frequently associated with each type

SENSING TYPES WITH THINKING (ST)	SENSING TYPES WITH FEELING (SF)
ISTJ Serious, quiet, earn success by concentration and thoroughness. Practical, orderly, matter-of-fact, logical, realistic, and dependable. See to it that everything is well organized. Take responsibility. Make up their own minds as to what should be accomplished and work toward it steadily, regardless of protests or distractions. Live their outer life more with thinking, inner more with *sensing*.	**ISFJ** Quiet, friendly, responsible, and conscientious. Work devotedly to meet their obligations. Lend stability to any project or group. Thorough, painstaking, accurate. Their interests are usually not technical. Can be patient with necessary details. Loyal, considerate, perceptive, concerned with how other people feel. Live their outer life more with feeling, inner more with *sensing*.
ISTP Cool onlookers – quiet, reserved, observing and analyzing life with detached curiosity and unexpected flashes of original humor. Usually interested in cause and effect, how and why mechanical things work, and in organizing facts using logical principles. Live their outer life more with sensing, inner more with *thinking*.	**ISFP** Retiring, quietly friendly, sensitive, kind modest about their abilities. Shun disagreements, do not force their opinions or values on others. Usually do not care to lead but are often loyal followers. Often relaxed about getting things done, because they enjoy the present moment and do not want to spoil it by undue haste or exertion. Live their outer life more with sensing, inner more with *feeling*.
ESTP Good at on-the-spot problem solving. Do not worry, enjoy whatever comes along. Tend to like mechanical things and sports, with friends on the side. Adaptable, tolerant, generally conservative in values. Dislike long explanations. Are best with real things that can be worked, handled, taken apart, or put together. Live their outer life more with *sensing*, inner more with thinking.	**ESFP** Outgoing, easygoing, accepting, friendly, enjoy everything and make things more fun for others by their enjoyment. Like sports and making things happen. Know what's going on and join in eagerly. Find remembering facts easier than mastering theories. Are best in situations that need sound common sense and practical ability with people as well as with things. Live their outer life more with *sensing*, inner more with feeling.
ESTJ Practical, realistic, matter-of-fact, with a natural head for business or mechanics. Not interested in subjects they see no use for, but can apply themselves when necessary. Like to organize and run activities. May make good administrators, especially if they remember to consider other people's feelings and points of view. Live their outer life more with *thinking*, inner more with sensing.	**ESFJ** Warmhearted, talkative, popular, conscientious, born cooperators, active committee members. Need harmony and may be good at creating it. Always doing something nice for someone. Work best with encouragement and praise. Main interest is in things that directly and visibly affect people's lives. Live their outer life more with *feeling*, inner more with sensing.

INTUITIVES WITH FEELING (NF)	INTUITIVES WITH THINKING (NT)
INFJ Succeed by perseverance, originality and desire to do whatever is needed or wanted. Put their best efforts into their work. Quietly forceful, conscientious, concerned for others. Respected for their firm principles. Likely to be honored and followed for their clear convictions as to how best to serve the common good. Live their outer life with more feeling, inner more with *intuition*.	**INTJ** Usually have original minds and great drive for their own ideas and purposes. In fields that appeal to them, they have a fine power to organize a job and carry it through with or without help. Skeptical, critical, independent, determined, sometimes stubborn. Must learn to yield less important points in order to win the most important. Live their outer life more with thinking, inner more with *intuition*.
INFP Full of enthusiasms and loyalties, but seldom talk of these until they know you well. Care about learning, ideas, language, and independent projects. Tend to undertake too much, then somehow get it done. Friendly, but often too absorbed in what they are doing to be sociable. Little concerned with possessions or physical surroundings. Live their outer life more with intuition, inner more with *feeling*.	**INTP** Quiet and reserved. Especially enjoy theoretical or scientific pursuits. Like solving problems with logic and analysis. Usually interested mainly in ideas, with little liking for parties or small talk. Tend to have sharply defined interests. Need careers where some strong interest can be used and useful. Live their outer life more with intuition, inner more with *thinking*.
ENFP Warmly enthusiatic, high-spirited, ingenious, imaginative. Able to do almost anything that interests them. Quick with a solution for any difficulty and ready to help anyone with a problem. Often rely on their ability to improvise instead of preparing in advance. Can usually find compelling reasons for whatever they want. Live their outer life more with *intuition*, inner more with feeling.	**ENTP** Quick, ingenious, good at many things. Stimulating company, alert and outspoken, may argue for fun on either side of a question. Resourceful in solving new and challenging problems, but may neglect routine assignments. Apt to turn to one new interest after another. Skillful in finding logical reasons for what they want. Live their outer life more with *intuition*, inner more with thinking.
ENFJ Responsive and responsible. Generally feel real concern for what others think or want, and try to handle things with due regard for the other person's feelings. Can present a proposal or lead a group discussion with ease and tact. Sociable, popular, sympathetic. Responsive to praise and criticism. Live their outer life more with *feeling*, inner more with intuition.	**ENTJ** Hearty, frank, decisive, leaders in activities. Usually good in anything that requires reasoning and intelligent talk, such as public speaking. Are well informed and enjoy adding to their fund of knowledge. May sometimes appear more positive and confident than their experience in an area warrants. Live their outer life more with *thinking*, inner more with intuition.

grief, we associate the functions of personality with the four energy resources as follows:

1. Sensing is related primarily to the physical resources.
2. Intuition is related primarily to the spiritual resources.
3. Thinking is related primarily to the intellectual resources.
4. Feeling is related primarily to the emotional resources.

These pairings will make it possible to discuss some powerful assumptions about how typical personality types may be affected by grief and how grief might affect people of the 16 types. Such a discussion may help you understand your own grief reaction and why it may be different from the way someone else might experience untimely grief. It also may help you manage the tasks of your grief process in a more constructive way.

Grief scrambles a person's world. It is only logical to assume that different people will respond in ways consistent with their personality strengths and weaknesses. The discussion to follow is based on our own analysis and from observing people in counseling and support groups. More research is needed in order to confirm that our theory and applications are scientifically valid and reliable. Gary offers seminars and workshops on "Personality and the Perception of Loss." For more information, contact Dr. Harbaugh personally.

For convenient reference, the 20 steps of grief model is repeated here so you can refer to it more easily during the following discussion.

Table 7.3. The 20 Steps Of Grief

Resources	Tasks				
	Acknowledge	Feel	Substitute	Detach	Reconstruct
Physical	1	5	9	13	17
Intellectual	2	6	10	14	18
Emotional	3	7	11	15	19
Spiritual	4	8	12	16	20

How Personality Preferences May Affect Grief

The S-N Scale

The *S* preference refers to people whose perception is based on the Sensing function while the *N* preference refers to people whose perception is based primarily on Intuition. *S* people look at life realistically and practically, while *N* people look beyond the facts to the imaginative possibilities those facts represent.

The *S* type person may be especially sensitive to the physical aspects of the grief process, those described in steps numbered 1, 5, 9, 13 and 17. When a spouse dies, the memory of the physical relationship may be strong. There may be especially keen feelings of deprivation of that physical relationship because physical presence plays a very important role in the life of the Sensing person. It would be a mistake, however, to think of the physical relationship as only sexual. The touch of the hand, the warmth of a hug, the sound of a voice, the smell of shaving lotion or perfume or of the couple's favorite meal cooking in the kitchen — any of these can be an important part of the physical relationship, in addition to sexual relations.

Actually, the Sensing person is observant of and responsive to any material, tangible connection with the spouse. The dead spouse's "things" are inseparable from the person who died and can be very painful reminders of the absent loved one. Disposing of these personal things may be very difficult and therefore may be delayed or avoided. Time may be needed for the Sensing person to get to the point of being able to part with the physical effects of the spouse.

In the pairing of MBTI personality preferences with the 20-step model above, you may have noticed that just as Sensing was paired with the Physical, so Intuition was paired with the Spiritual. We need to comment on this. Since Intuition is the opposite of Sensing, it might seem that we are saying the Intuitives are spiritual and Sensing persons are not. That would not be true. *Every personality type can have a spiritual outlook and no one MBTI type is necessarily more spiritually-minded than the others.* However, the Sensing person's spirituality is more likely to be connected with concrete here and now realities.

Gary has written about the spirituality of the different MBTI types in a recent book titled, *God's Gifted People.* (See references.) What may happen is that the Sensing person's preferred approach to spirituality could be more difficult to sustain in the face of death since death shatters the immediate physical relationship with the spouse. The Intuition that might offer some spiritual comfort by relocating the relationship to another dimension of intimacy is usually one of the lesser-developed functions of the Sensing person. Therefore, into the situation of darkness caused by the death, Sensing persons have less light from Intuition, since Intuition is for them an opening to the darker, less conscious side.

N types may be more open to the subconscious and unconscious spiritual aspects of grief, those described in steps numbered 4, 8, 12, 16 and 20. The *N* type person may feel spiritually bonded to the spouse in spite of the physical loss. While there may be comfort in this, the Intuitive may be much less in touch with the practicalities of life or the means to handle them. The whole area of self-care seems to be more of a problem to Intuitives than it may be for Sensing types. If the spouse who died was a Sensing person, probably that spouse took care of many of the day-to-day needs, perhaps financial as well as physical. The Intuitive may overlook the obvious physical (Sensing) aspects of life which need attention. This may include such basics as meals and keeping up with ongoing bills.

The T-F Scale

The *T* preference leads to decision-making that is based more on logical reasoning. The *F* preference describes people who emphasize the values and feelings of themselves and others in making decisions. Remember that we said both are rational processes but each has its own rationale.

T people will probably do a lot of thinking in the grief process. They may analyze the life they shared with their spouse and the consequences of their spouse's death. They may probe into and even do research on the cause of the death in an effort to understand the reasons why death occurred. Thinking persons usually think ahead and take a long-range view of things. Sometimes their tendency to analyze things makes them appear to others to be unemotional and detached from the process of grief.

T people may have difficulty dealing with the more emotional aspects of grief. The Feeling side of their personality is usually less developed. Thinking persons will also typically be befuddled and confused by a death which doesn't make sense. They assume a certain logical order to life and when untimely grief destroys their logic they may fear the loss of their moorings. They will probably be most at home handling the intellectual aspects of grief described in steps 2, 6, 10, 14 and 18 and probably least confident with the emotional challenges.

The opposite is true of Feeling people. *F* people seek harmony in their lives and in their relationships with others. They may miss the good times with their spouse but feel guilty at not missing the bad times. They may feel their emotions of grief more naturally and be able to work them through because they are usually more willing to experience those feelings — which is the prerequisite for working them through. Areas of readjustment requiring logical thinking may cause them concern. They might just avoid dealing with such things as analyzing their current financial situation or logically thinking out the pros and cons of moving and the possible consequences of other major changes. They may also be more susceptible to unethical or pseudo caregivers and others who can defraud them emotionally as well as financially. They generally have a trusting nature and will approach new relationships with open arms, possibly to their own detriment. They will probably be most sensitive to the emotional factors described in steps 3, 7, 11, 15 and 19.

Linking Personality Functions With Resources

We have now discussed the four major personality functions, Sensing, Intuition, Thinking and Feeling. They are the four personality processes most centrally involved in a grief reaction because the four combinations (ST, SF, NF, NT) lead to very different ways of seeing life and to different ways of making decisions. When the death of a spouse occurs, our habitual way of seeing things causes us to see some things and miss some others. Until our usual ways of deciding no longer work, we go about decision-making in ways that are the most familiar to us and use our preferred functions in typical ways.

Each of the 16 possible personality type combinations results in a particular ordering or priority of personality preferences that are likely to show up in the coping process of grief. The particular order of preferences for a given individual may help to explain the way that particular person manages (or will manage) the stress encountered in the process of recovery as well as that person's order of reliance on physical, intellectual, emotional and spiritual reactions.

The following tables show the ranking of the functions for the various types, related to the resources. To interpret the tables, you just apply the numerical priorities assigned to each of the resources as discussed in the previous text. In this way, the various functions

of personality are related to the 20 steps of grief model more explic-
itly. The numerical priorities rank the preferences of the individual
types in terms of the resources of the model. For example, ESTP
persons whose Dominant is sensing and whose Inferior or least-
preferred function is Intuition may find their greatest resource in the
physical realm (1) and their greatest uncertainty and limitation in
coping resources in the spiritual realm (4).

Much more research is needed in this area, but the work we have
done so far indicates this linkage is extremely useful in analyzing
how the personality functions affect and are affected by grief. It may
help you to know how your own functions rank so you can understand a little better why you may feel as you do. It may not make the
suffering any less but knowing something about why you are react-
ing as you are can help you feel a little more comfortable and reduce
some of the fear and anxiety that can be disabling. Keeping in mind
that everyone is an individual and no "chart" is 100 percent true for
everyone, you may find it helpful to locate what you think might be
your type in the tables that follow and then reread the text sections
on each type of grief with a renewed emphasis on how that task
might be affected by your personality preferences. In this way you
can tailor this book to your unique personality.

A Look At The Other Scales

The two others scales of the MBTI (E-I and J-P) are also useful in
anticipating how a person might experience grief and how that
person might handle a loss once it has occurred. First, let's look at
the E-I Scale.

The E-I Scale

The *E* refers to extraverted preferences while the *I* refers to introverted preferences. In everyday life Extraverts enjoy and like to
be involved in the outer world of people and things. When a loss
occurs, *E* people may want others around and as soon as possible
want to get involved again with activities. Extraverts seem to be
more drawn to support groups and group travel opportunities, the
kinds of things that get them outside themselves. They may busy
themselves with volunteer or avocational activities that will provide
the needed contact with people and things. If they are forced to live
alone, their quiet times can get quite lonely. Sometimes they may
walk through shopping malls just for the contact with people and
the bustle they can enjoy there.

Table 7.4
Linking The Extraverted And Sensing Types With Resources

Resources	ESTP	ESFP	ESTJ	ESFJ
Physical	1	1	2	2
Intellectual	2	3	1	4
Emotional	3	2	4	1
Spiritual	4	4	3	3

Table 7.5
Linking The Extraverted And Intuitive Types With Resources

Resources	ENFP	ENTP	ENFJ	ENTJ
Physical	4	4	3	3
Intellectual	3	2	4	1
Emotional	2	3	1	4
Spiritual	1	1	2	2

Table 7.6
Linking The Introverted And Sensing Types With Resources

Resources	ISTJ	ISFJ	ISTP	ISFP
Physical	1	1	2	2
Intellectual	2	3	1	4
Emotional	3	2	4	1
Spiritual	4	4	3	3

Table 7.7
Linking The Introverted And Intuitive Types With Resources

Resources	INFJ	INTJ	INFP	INTP
Physical	4	4	3	3
Intellectual	3	2	4	1
Emotional	2	3	1	4
Spiritual	1	1	2	2

They will probably be very aware of the absence of their spouse when doing (or asked to do) something they always did as a couple. Extraverts enjoy talking and will miss conversation times with their spouse if there was good communication between them. When the *E* person wants to talk, it will likely be about people and things and events and activities. People with the *E* preference are very responsive to what is going on around them. If they do not experience adequate support from their environment, Extraverts are likely to become all the more depressed.

The Introverted person typically is not drawn to large group activities because the Introvert's energy does not come from outside but rather from inner resources. If a spouse dies, the Introvert may not naturally reach out for the support of other people or want to get involved in outside activities, even though it might be helpful to do so. It is not that the support of other people is unimportant to Introverts (in fact, it may be crucial to their mental health) but rather that reaching out is not the usual approach of the *I*. When in group situations, the Introvert may be quiet and appear to be outside of the group. However, the Introvert may feel much more of a connection with the group than is apparent to others.

An Introvert tends to be reflective by nature. When a death occurs, the *I* will probably spend a good bit of time contemplating the loss and its meaning. This can be depressing as there is a limit to the kinds of answers that can come from within. An Introvert may be more likely than an Extravert to research the illness or cause of death of the spouse and may be more motivated to read books on the subject of death and grief.

Social support is important to the *I,* but social support probably will be defined as involving one or two or at most a few close friends. With these trusted friends the *I* may talk freely, something that would usually be much more uncomfortable for the Introvert to do in a large group setting. Consequently, one of the primary supports for bereaved persons, a group of persons who have had a similar experience, may not have the immediate appeal to an Introvert that it might for an Extravert. If someone the Introvert knows and trusts goes to such a group, that person may be able to extend an invitation that will have a better chance of being accepted.

An interesting question that needs more research before there can be an answer is whether Extraverts and Introverts have different vulnerabilities to the kinds of physical and emotional problems that sometimes follow the loss of a spouse. It would seem possible that anxiety and depression would arise when the usual (and different) ways that Extraverts and Introverts have their needs met are frustrated by the death of the partner. It is not that an *I* will become depressed and *E* will not (or vice versa), but rather that they are likely to become depressed by different things or events.

It is possible there is also a different susceptibility rate to physical complaints that may accompany bereavement. Extraverts seem to be more outer-directed, Introverts seems to be more inner-directed. Are certain kinds of physical symptoms more likely to be experienced by virtue of these differences? If it were possible to identify the stressors and the probable consequences, preventative steps might be taken by family and caregivers to offset some of the problems that occur during the grieving process. We believe the perspective offered by the MBTI can be helpful in researching these questions.

The J-P Scale

As we said earlier, people whose MBTI type ends in the letter *J* usually show to the outside world their preferred decision-making function, Thinking or Feeling. People whose type ends with the letter *P* show their way of perceiving to the outside world, which is either Sensing or Intuition. Extraverts show to the outside world their most preferred (Dominant) function. Introverts show to others their second most preferred (Auxiliary) function. The Introvert's Dominant is kept inside, in the favored inner world.

Judging *(J)* people prefer closure and control. They like to be on top of their situation. *J* persons may be perceived as responsible because they set goals and deadlines and do their best to meet those commitments punctually. They typically do not like surprises or changes that alter their basic approach to life. They do not like open-ended situations. Since death wrests control away from them, the loss can be especially disconcerting and unbalancing. They can experience anger and fear as long as uncertainty about their future continues. They need to find ways of regaining some control and order in their lives as soon as possible to avoid general depression.

If their preferred function is Thinking (___TJ), Judging persons may feel total frustration and a sense of befuddlement if they are unable to rationalize a new plan for their lives. If they prefer Feeling (___FJ), and especially if they are also Extraverted (E_FJ), they may seek to avoid the pain of grief by making a premature decision. Do certain types like the E___J or the E_FJ want closure so badly that they are more likely to mistake substitution for Reconstruction? Would they be more vulnerable to reconnecting with someone without waiting for the working through of the grief process? Whatever the effect of the different combinations turns out to be, it is fair to say that *J* people generally want to get their lives back in order and under control as soon as possible and are extremely frustrated when they cannot. They want to move toward Reconstruction and usually appreciate assistance that helps them regain a sense of being on top of their situation.

Perceiving people *(P)* show to the outside world their way of perceiving rather than their way of judging, so they appear to be more flexible and adaptable. Typically, they find schedules and deadlines constraining. They prefer to approach life in a more open-ended way. They would rather not come to closure too soon. So as not to close off any option, a *P* will continue to gather information rather than risk a premature conclusion.

Just as a *J* may want to move too quickly toward Substitution and possibly confuse it with Reconstruction, a *P* may also have some personality-related problems during the grief process. We are researching whether the *P* personality is more likely to have difficulty with detachment. Since death has imposed a closure on the relationship with their spouse, the Perceiving person may find it more difficult to accept the death as an absolute end. It may take longer for the *P* to be ready to enter Reconstruction, since Reconstruction necessitates acknowledging the death as an ending. In order to move on to the new possibilities inherent in Reconstruction, the Perceiving person will need to work hard at giving up the attachment to the spouse.

P people who also prefer Sensing are likely to approach the tasks of grief on a day-to-day basis with not as much thought for the future. They may need help and motivation to make needed plans for their future lifestyle and security. If they are not financially secure, their future can be fairly uncertain.

P people who prefer Intuition can be ingeniously creative but they may need some help in practical matters of life such as banking or setting up a budget. Each of the other personality traits, Extraversion and Introversion, Thinking and Feeling, will also affect how the *P* person handles grief. Theoretically, an E___P person is more likely to do something spontaneously than the opposite type, I___J. An INTP is more likely to have difficulty with the emotional steps of grief than an ENFP.

By following our descriptions of the different personality characteristics, you can anticipate that any particular combination will be faced with a particular challenge and have certain typical reactions during the grief process.

You now have a brief description of how personality types may affect and be affected by the grief process. As we said earlier, we all make some use of every one of the personality gifts. However, some are preferred by each individual. Our particular combination of preferences helps make us the special person that we are. As we get older we may make a more balanced use of both sides of each scale, although we remain true to our own natural (Jung called it "innate") preference with which we entered the world and which we chose to develop.

Our premise is that, when we are faced with a major loss, we react as the whole person that we are. The personality patterns with which we approach other areas of life are also going to be involved in how we experience and handle grief. Knowing why we experience grief as we do may give us some clues as to what we need to do to move along in the process (or what it might take to help someone else during the time of their grieving). We hope you now have a better idea why we recommend that you try to find a way of determining your own particular personality type preferences so you can use this powerful tool to help manage your grief process more effectively.

You may have guessed that some personality types seem to have more coping resources than others when it comes to managing crisis situations. Such a conclusion is also suggested in preliminary research reported to the 1989 conference of the Association for Psychological Type by Dr. Allen Hammer of Consulting Psychologists Press.

Dr. Hammer correlated the scores of his sample groups on the Coping Resources Inventory (CRI) with the MBTI types and came up with the table which follows. The CRI is a questionnaire developed by Dr. Hammer and M. Susan Marting to mearsure the cognitive, social, spiritual, emotional and physical resources that a person has for coping with stress. The results showed a consistent pattern across all the sample groups. The way to read table 7.8 is as follows:

- "Number" means the number of person preferring each type. For example there were 112 persons in this study of which 11 indicated a preference for ENFP.
- "Total" means the relative ranking when the uses of *all* coping resources were taken into consideration. In this sample ENFPs seem to have the most resources, INTPs the fewest.
- The other columns show a particular type's ranking compared with the other types on each of the scales (cognitive, social,

emotional, spiritual, physical). In this sample ENFPs rank highest on all scales except the spiritual where INFJs rank highest.

Table 7.8. Rankings By The 16 Types On CRI Scales

	Number	Total	Cognitive	Social	Emotional	Spiritual	Physical
ENFP	11	1	1	1	1	2	1
INFJ	15	2	2	6	5	1	4
ENTJ	13	3	3	5	4	3	2
ESFP	2	3	2	2	5	4	5
ISFJ	4	3	2	5	5	2	3
ENTP	6	4	3	5	3	5	6
ESTJ	4	5	1	4	2	8	6
ISTP	3	6	5	10	5	4	5
ESFJ	5	7	7	6	6	2	9
ENFJ	2	8	4	3	9	4	7
ISFP	2	8	6	7	6	1	10
INFP	4	9	3	8	8	2	8
INTJ	18	10	3	10	7	3	8
ISTJ	12	11	4	9	8	6	7
INTP	11	12	6	10	10	7	5

Note: There were no ESTP's in this sample.

Although Dr. Hammer's findings need to be confirmed by additional research with larger numbers of subjects, still there are implications for individuals coping with stress. In general, special attention may need to be directed toward identifying introverts who may not be coping well and in helping them develop more effective coping strategies and resources. This may be especially needed by those who ranked low on the "total" CRI scores (for example, INTP and ISTJ ranked 11th and 12th). Clinical experience using the Coping Resources Inventory has suggested that intervention aimed at helping individuals deal with stress should be directed toward helping them identify and bring into use the full range of resources available to them.

Of course, we have also tried to make it clear that the process of grief is affected by more than our personality type. The nature of our relationship with our spouse, our value system, social experiences, cultural modes and early life development, as well as the physical, intellectual, emotional and social realities of our life also affect the way we grieve. So does our sense of the overall meaning and purpose of life (spirituality). We believe personality factors are a very important part of the picture. We encourage you to think carefully about how knowledge of these personality factors may be of help to you. You might start by keeping the MBTI personality preferences in mind as you now turn to the next chapter, "Creating And Maintaining New Relationships."

8

Creating And Maintaining New Relationships

Most married couples know, if they stop to think about it, that one of them is likely to die before the other. If death comes prematurely, the one who is left has years — perhaps many years — of life ahead. Facing life as a couple is one thing, but how does a surviving husband or wife re-enter the social world without the one who has been such an integral part of day-to-day living — especially when that social world has so drastically changed?

In the discussion that follows, we are going to present a variety of ways in which those who have lost a spouse can try to manage their return to active social life. The issues we discuss are real and must be dealt with by all survivors in a way consistent with their beliefs and values.

If you reached 21 years of age prior to 1965, you will probably encounter a way of life among modern sin-

gles that is much different than you are used to. Adapting to that
single life can be a fearful experience. Four major social develop-
ments occurred during the last half of the sixties that have had a
revolutionary impact on lifestyles ever since: the availability of the
birth control pill, legal interpretation of freedom of the press to
permit a more open, liberal portrayal of sex in the media; the
challenge to authority growing out of the controversy over the Viet-
nam war; and the economic and social impact of the Women's
Liberation movement.

Post-World War II

In the post-World War II period, the ideal lifestyle to initiate as
soon as possible after high school was considered to include romantic love, marriage and the beginning of a family. This model
may have served as a correction to the disruption caused by the war
and previous economic depression periods. But marriage was sometimes entered prematurely with some living a life of frustration and
isolation because divorce was not as acceptable a solution to marital
problems as it is now.

Many of those who remained married lost sight of the social
changes taking place all around them. The traditional social pattern
was slowly but surely being replaced with a wide variety of alternative lifestyles. If you were raised by traditional parents and grew up
during the time we have described, your re-entry into single life is
likely to be marked by emotional and value conflicts pulling you in
several different directions.

The 1990s

In today's singles world, there are temporary relationships, short-
term relationships and long-term relationships — committed and
uncommitted. Within these relationships the degree of intimacy
varies. Our modern geographic mobility and changing economy
now forces many of us to search for intimacy in more short-term
relationships without the luxury of traditional long-term commitments. These *ad hoc*, "disposable" relationships are prized by some
as a way to gain new insights and perceptions in varied and unres-
tricted situations without mutual dependencies. However, the price
may be the loss of traditional feelings of responsible love and the
security which we obtained in the more rooted society of the past.

Given this situation, recovering mid-life singles have a choice of
pulling back or entering into this unfamiliar world. Both options

are painful but a choice must be made. In life there is no such thing as simply standing still.

Dr. Morris Massey, referenced by Michael D. Yapko, has observed that people develop 90 percent of their basic values by age 10 and the rest by age 20. How we come to view life (including its social, political, religious, economic and family aspects) during that period tends to stay with us the rest of our lives. These perspectives tend to endure. According to Charles Whitfield, the inner child of your past still exists and drives your life as an adult. You must learn to be a respectful parent to that child within you. Massey said values can be changed but it usually takes a "significant emotional event" to stimulate the motivation to change basic beliefs. Certainly, the loss of your spouse and the task of social reconstruction can be such an event.

Generational Differences

People who matured in the decade of the 1960s may have a different set of values from those maturing in the 1950s and 1970s. Their tastes in music, religion, politics and lifestyle may be different. They may bring differing patterns of behavior to their relationships. Carol Becker, Ruth Westheimer and Louis Lieberman have described the anxiety and changes brought about by the transitional roles of men and women in our culture since the end of World War II and the implications this has had for lifestyles, morals and ethics.

Absolute authority for what was believed to be "good," "bad," "right" and "wrong" is being questioned and repositioned in many areas of life. Your own beliefs about moral standards may be called into question and may need to be re-evaluated in light of the new reality of your life. Wayne Dyer suggests that instead of being victimized by the "good-bad," "right-wrong" judgments, it is better to think of "healthy/unhealthy," "legal/illegal," "effective/ineffective," "works/doesn't work," which are reality-based and can have more real meaning in your life. He says you must decide for yourself, not only whether behavior is right or wrong, but whether it is effective in helping you achieve legitimate moral and ethical goals. He challenges us to be aware of our beliefs, test them against reality and adopt new beliefs that are more reality-based as well as self-enhancing.

Other Changes

Other changes in single male-female relationships that you will need to understand and adapt to are explained by Tracy Cabot, and by Sonya Rhodes and Marlin S. Potash. Their books were written by women about men but they can be helpful to men as well. They provide an excellent description of the new forms of relationships that have developed during the decades of the 1970s and 1980s.

Cabot discusses modern dating and the communications styles that can lead from casual dating to commitment. Rhodes and Potash comment on the difficulty many people today have with making a lifetime commitment to another. Both of these issues will have a lot to do with the success or failure of your attempts to reconnect and possibly make a new life with another person. Along the way there will be many opportunities for making mistakes.

If you concentrated your social life exclusively within your marriage, especially if you are an Introvert, making new social contacts now can be quite uncomfortable. As with other new skills, it gets easier with practice. So if you can make the attempt to meet new people, confidence and motivation should follow.

Cabot suggests that if you want a new relationship, you should write out a description of the ideal person you seek. The description should include all the aspects of any new relationship that are important to you in terms of the model of the whole person used in this book: physical, intellectual, emotional and spiritual. This, then, must be combined with the four elements of your preferred lifestyle in terms of professional, social, personal and private dimensions.

Things That Get In The Way

We'll come back to Cabot's suggestion, but it is important here to think about some things that could get in the way of making the most of what Cabot says. For example, some people are attracted to those who can fill the gaps in their own makeup, those who tend to make them feel whole and complete. This need may arise from their relations with their parents during childhood, from basic personality needs of both. Kevin Leman and Pia Mellody described several faulty parenting behaviors that warp a child's sense of self-worth and can set one up for a life of painful attempts to overcome them. There are perfectionist parents who are strong on performance, discipline and criticism; authoritarian parents who are always on the child's back, barking orders and commands; overpermissive and oversubmissive parents who let the child rule the roost; overindulgent parents who substitute gifts for love; abusive parents who both physically and verbally motivate with guilt and fear; neglectful parents who don't share feelings and just can't be bothered with their children; and rejecting parents who literally refuse to accept their children. Parents who are dysfunctional or unavailable due to alcohol, chronic illness or other problems contribute to the development of what is now known as co-dependent behavior.

We have used the word co-dependent a number of times. In the context of our discussion of the development of new relationships, perhaps it would be well to say again that a co-dependent person is one who has developed a certain behavior that makes it difficult to maintain functional, healthy, fulfilling relationships with others. Through reactions to trauma, emptiness and dysfunctional relationships with family and close intimates, co-dependents learn to use others (mates, friends, even children) as a source of identity, value and well-being. They try to restore within themselves the emotional losses of childhood as a way of surviving. It is a deep-rooted compulsive behavior derived from a sometimes moderately and sometimes extremely dysfunctional family system, often related to alcoholism, drug abuse or chronic illness. Pia Mellody, Melody Beattie and many other writers are now addressing the issues raised by co-dependency. Elements of such faulty behaviors may be part of the baggage a person may carry that needs to be overcome in relations with others.

Position In The Family

There are other factors that influence present-day relationships. Leman believes birth order has a lot to do with our adult behavior. First-borns and only children are usually perfectionistic, reliable, conscientious, critical, serious and scholarly. They are eager to please, goal oriented and respectful of authority. Middle children tend to be mediators, conflict avoiders and independent, with extreme loyalty to their peer group and many friends. Last borns are often charming, able to avoid blame, "people" persons, good in sales, precocious and engaging.

Opposite-Sex Parent

We often are also attracted to people who represent the ideal image of the opposite-sex parent, what we believe the perfect father or mother would be like. If these images are flawed due to painful life experiences, then we may be attracted to people who have problems. It may take the help of a therapist to dig out the real reasons why you prefer certain types of people in your intimate, private life. In this connection, another interesting perspective is offered by Daryl Sharp. Sharp discusses Jung's theory that we have opposite sexual elements in our own personalities (which Jung called the anima and the animus) that, at an unconscious level, also help to determine who is attractive to us.

Family Assumptions

If your marriage was based upon a faulty assumption about your self-worth, now may be the time to work on improving your self-image as you decide what you are seeking in a new partner or group of friends. You can also become more aware of personalities, your own and those of others, and the implications of personality for new relationships. In the last chapter we pointed out that certain personality types tend to come to conclusions quickly, wanting to finalize decisions even before they have considered all the alternatives. Others find it difficult to come to closure, preferring to keep their options open. If you have not already done so, now may be a good time to find a qualified counselor who can administer the Myers-Briggs Type Indicator to you and interpret the result so you will understand yourself and others better. The final chapter in Gary's *God's Gifted People* describes the use of the MBTI as it applies to relationships.

Choosing An Ideal Partner

Now let's return to Cabot's suggestions. With a description of your ideal partner in hand, you will have a guide to decision-making as you make new social encounters. It may not be possible to meet all your requirements among the people available to you but this exercise can help to focus your attention on people more likely to be compatible. It can help you avoid painful situations arising from otherwise faulty choices that you may have to undo after making a considerable emotional investment.

Due to the many lifestyles now socially accepted, it may be more difficult to choose a suitable partner than it was in your youth. You might try to recall in some detail the social, political, economic, religious and family aspects of life during your teenage years and do the same in your own mind about the people you sense as potential partners. This will help you understand them and your new relationships better. The great changes in social values that occurred in the 1960s cause people who matured in the 1950s to behave considerably differently in dating from those who matured in the 1970s and later.

Many women who matured after 1970 seem to have adapted readily to their new freedoms and equality with men, while many men are still restricted by the traditional sexual roles of the past.

Many of both sexes are caught in the conflict between their traditional upbringing and the new liberal lifestyles. If you were married and out of the singles life during this period of major social changes, you may find it difficult to adjust to the changed social life and less inhibited dating behavior that you may now encounter as a newly single person.

Jed Diamond wrote that social conditioning in our culture still tends to program males and females differently. Leman says the five major needs of men and woman are basically different. For men, they are sexual fulfillment, recreational companionship, an attractive spouse, domestic support and admiration. For women, they are affection, conversation, honesty and openness, financial support and family commitment. No wonder Diamond notes that one of the ironies of life is that the sexes are rarely in tune with each other!

Platonic Friendships

To get a better handle on all these changes and differences, perhaps the best route for you at first is to develop some platonic friendships. Not only will this clarify some of your thinking, but also such friendships are an excellent way of boosting your self-esteem and of feeling the benefits of being needed and useful to somebody else. That way you get the much needed practice in getting reacquainted with your own new self and situation.

Letty Pogrebin estimated there are 70 million single adults in this country. Many of them report a lack of nurturing friendships, although most people have plenty of acquaintances. Women seem to have more close friends than men do, possibly because men are taught to be more competitive, strong and self-reliant. However, women who are professional and career-oriented often find it difficult to make close women friends.

Pogrebin reported that history shows it to be extremely difficult, although not impossible, for platonic friendships to be maintained between opposite sexes. Her findings indicate that men need women more than women need men for maintenance of self-esteem. And although half of all friendships occur between people within five years of the same age, beautiful and fruitful friendships can be developed with people of all ages. Both sexes can benefit from having three to five close friends of either sex especially after age 40 or so as families begin to move toward the "empty nest." However they are based, solid friendships are worth developing.

Pogrebin defined platonic relationships in degrees of closeness: acquaintances, neighbors, confederates, pals, close kin, co-workers and friends. A true friend is someone who exhibits loyalty and trust, is generous with time, effort, acceptance and money, is truthful, open and honest. Necessary ingredients of friendship include physical proximity, similarity (remember the proverb, "Birds of a feather flock together."), reciprocal liking and openness about self-disclosure.

Although romance and sex are enhanced by friendship, friendship is often affected by romance and sex. The greeting of a platonic friend warms the heart; when it quickens the loins the rules change. When a friendship crosses that line it becomes something else.

At this point in your life, having an intimate relationship with only one person at the expense of other friendly attachments is risky and very narrowing. Halpern pointed out that no one can meet all of our needs completely, so if we have multiple sources for meeting our needs, we will be more independent, secure and free. This does not mean all our attachments must have equal meaning. It is not only possible but highly desirable to be deeply devoted to a primary partner and still have much of your need for connectedness met by other friends, close kin, colleagues, co-workers and others.

Also, as Halpern has warned, we should not base our relationships on the need to meet a co-dependent attachment hunger derived from insufficient or flawed parenting that did not permit us to develop a healthy adult sense of self-worth and independence. There *is* a healthy form of attachment hunger but we can be addicted to the need for intimacy with another human being if our separation from parents was never emotionally completed.

It is not healthy for anyone to rush into new intimate relationships to replace a lost spouse, especially if the marriage had some elements of co-dependency. It is better to work out this problem first, with professional help. Then it may be time to consider a romantic relationship.

How A New Relationship Evolves

Judith Sills has explained that new relationships evolve through a rather standard set of phases. The first activity is a selection process, which is itself a form of ritual in our society. Subtle and not so subtle forms of flirting or body language are used to express an interest in someone who appeals to our senses.

After contact is made, deciding whether this will be a more serious relationship usually takes a little time, perhaps a month or more. At the end of this time, the one pursued may react positively, only to find the pursuer turning cold and withdrawing. The one sought might then become the seeker. This phase can take a month or two to resolve. If it is resolved, the relationship actually begins and the two individuals become a couple.

The relationship then may proceed to a plateau. The couple may enjoy each other physically and emotionally, begin to feel in love and fantasize about the future together. Then comes a time of negotiating the resolution of inevitable differences which leads to a final phase of commitment or a breakup. This may be two years or more after the beginning of the selection. Some couples stay deadlocked in negotiations for years, others move on to marriage and some resolve into a less conventional lifestyle at various levels of intimacy.

This process of mid-life courtship is full of anxiety and ambiguity for both parties. It can be quite energy-consuming for older people with the complex of life experiences they bring to the process. In widowed situations there is the additional complication of resolving guilt over being unfaithful. This may linger even though detachment from the deceased spouse has mostly been completed. If you are still emotionally attached to your dead spouse, guilt may be a strong factor. Unless this is overcome you can be on a rocky road.

You may not be able to tell exactly why, where, when or with whom you may fall in love again but you can be aware of your personal boundaries and to a great extent you can control your actions in response. Be aware of your vulnerability if your personal boundaries are not respected. Loving does not mean being victim-ized and you should avoid being drawn into relationships with people who might want to exploit you. You can also learn to avoid becoming too emotionally invested in people who respond to you only out of their own dependency or attachment needs.

Your success at going from casual dating to monogamous dating, to more serious commitment and possibly marriage depends a great deal on how effective you are at making real contact with the other person. This, in turn, depends upon the compatibility of your re-spective communicating styles.

How People Communicate

People communicate in a variety of ways. Your MBTI personality type is usually reflected in the kind of communication that comes most naturally to you. In addition, people are likely to use their senses of sight, hearing and touch in certain ways. As intimacy develops, we tend to concentrate our response on the sense that is most important to us. At the outset of a new contact, the most preferred sense is usually the one that grabs or hooks us into getting closer. It might be the sight, sound or touch of the person, how she or he looks, talks or feels. The person may remind you in some way of your lost spouse or even of a previous love from your youthful single life. Or it may be a person with characteristics opposite from your experiences who is most attractive now.

As a new relationship develops, differences or similarities in communications preference can pull the couple closer toward shared intimacy or push them apart. It is possible to learn how to meet the core communications needs of the other person, responding to their core needs in every type of situation from casual dating to sexual encounters.

If you can be aware of your own preference and can tell your partner's communication priority, you can modify your approach in order to meet the other person's needs. In fact, you will have to use compatible communications styles for the relationship to develop into full commitment. For example, if your partner is an Extravert oriented to audible communcation and you are Introverted, you will need to concentrate on being more verbally communicative if you value the relationship and want it to last.

If your partner prefers visual stimulation, you may need to provide dinners by candlelight, scenic encounters and conversation that emphasizes visual images. Even the type of pictures on your walls or the clothes you wear can make a difference in the level of intimacy you achieve with a visually oriented person. If your partner prefers touch, you may need to be more physically demonstrative and use tactile images in your conversation.

You can drive your partner away if you insist on meeting your own communications priorities without adapting to hers or his. If you prefer to talk, see sights or be physical and your partner prefers another approach, you may abort the relationship without either partner understanding why. People who make decisions based on Thinking may later figure it out, but people who base decisions on Feeling may just walk away, turned off. The key to successful intimate communications is to be sensitive to the clues, spoken and unspoken, given by your partner so you can respond with the preferred type of communications behavior.

Jean Kummerow has written a brief overview of how to "talk in Type," using an understanding of the personality differences identifed by the MBTI. You might find it helpful. Hopefully, in your communication, your partner will be as eager to please you.

What About Sex?

If you become active in the modern dating world and have the opportunity of getting together in private with your partner, you may also have to decide what to do about sex. Moral values in our culture concerning sexual relations between consenting adults now range from permissive (purely uncommitted, recreational sex) to conservative religious views which sanction sexual relations only in marriage. Whether or not you find a new sexual relationship satisfying outside of marriage has roots deep in your value system and your religious training, as well as your cultural circumstances and your overall orientation to life.

Even among those whose value system grew out of Christian teaching, there is a wide variety of popular opinion about what may be right or wrong in sexuality between consenting adults. There is a considerable divergence of opinion among the various religious denominations, depending upon how one chooses to interpret the Bible. Whatever you decide for yourself, your decision is likely to be better if it is based on a concept of wholeness, involving the intellectual, emotional and spiritual as well as the physical aspects.

Because of their circumstances or their beliefs, many widows and widowers find their need for sexual fulfillment very difficult to meet. Books by Richard Walters and by Ruth Westheimer and Louis Lieberman attempt to make the case for a more liberal and nonjudgmental approach to sexual behavior based on the ethics of each situation. With all the divergent views now existing in our culture, each of us must be responsible for our own actions. Invitation or pressure for casual sex from your new liberated friends may create depression and anxiety if it violates your traditional standards, based on religion, laws or psychological and emotional development. The result is called cognitive dissonance, or a lack of harmony or agreement between belief and action, a discordant, incompatible, incongruous situation. Keep in mind the potential for mental suffering in sexual relationships if your partner takes a less committed, more casual approach to sex than your values support.

If you are to avoid painful emotional conflicts, you may need to change your values to match your behavior or control your behavior to match your values. Be aware that it is not easy to change basic values, if your values are really your own. In any case, sex as a way of replacing your self-esteem should be avoided. It won't work.

Hajcak and Garwood identified 18 different nonsexual emotional factors that can distort and blunt the sexual act and interfere with

healthy relationships. Both you and your partner may bring nonsexual baggage into the bedroom. These issues should be discussed
openly and solved outside of the sexual relationship. Nonsexual
factors that cannot appropriately be met in sexual relations, and thus
cause unsatisfying results, should be identified and removed from
the bedroom. They are:

- sex to gain affection
- sex to avoid intimacy
- sex to avoid loneliness
- sex for atonement
- sex to safeguard fidelity
- sex to confirm sexuality
- sex to build self-esteem
- sex to overcome guilt
- sex to mask anger
- sex to control
- sex for revenge
- sex to overcome jealousy
- sex to overcome boredom
- sex to dominate
- sex as a haven
- sex for social pleasure
- sex to buffer depression
- sex as rebellion.

If any of these objectives are carried into the bedroom, even
though subconsciously, they will confuse the sex act and neither the
nonsexual objective nor sexual needs will be satisfied. Both sexual
and nonsexual needs will be frustrated and the relationship will be
flawed. A careful analysis may disclose that you carry over some of
them from your marriage, unresolved and still powerful enough to
mar any new relationship. If you are a traditional person, sexual
relations outside marriage may cause conflict if your value system
and your behavior are not consistent.

What About Commitment?

It is also well to remember that engaging in sex and making a
commitment are not the same thing. Rhodes and Potash explain that
coming to commitment in modern times is more of a process of
growing together than a specific sexual event. Commitment evolves
from the overall value one places on his or her investment in the

relationship: physical, intellectual, emotional and spiritual. This is a change from the social situation prior to the mid-1960s, when it was more likely that commitment was black and white, when "going steady" was marked by prolonged kissing or petting and formal commitment was marked by exchanging class rings or initiating sexual relations.

Since purely physical or recreational sex outside of marriage is now so readily accepted among many singles, it is no longer a reliable measure of commitment. In fact, being lovers may be less significant than being friends to some. People with this belief may feel that having hormone-driven, recreational sex with casual friends does not require any significant commitment.

This attitude may represent a substantial and painful departure from traditional thinking if you are more conservative or if your religious beliefs suggest sexual relating is more meaningful than contemporary behavior seems to suggest. If you place a high value on a sexual friendship, becoming attached to a person with a more casual attitude can cause considerable suffering if commensurate commitment is not forthcoming as you might expect and want.

For purposes of analyzing commitment, Rhodes and Potash classify single people in three categories — good enough, good today/gone tomorrow and good for nothing! Needless to say, the commitment level is different in each case. Rhodes and Potash then identify five levels of discernible commitment. The five levels they identify with commitment are:

1. Open dating, possibly with recreational sex, with several partners and zero commitment
2. Steady dating, most likely with some "meaningful" sex
3. A monogamous form of publicly going steady and having sex with only that person
4. Monogamy-plus where the families and friends of the couple are brought into the relationship
5. Open commitment and possibly living together with intentions of getting married.

If you are not very experienced, you can easily confuse the behavior of your lower level partner with a more advanced level of commitment.

Another complication is that two people often are not on the same level at the same time. Both parties can drift forward and backward in the levels at their own pace, for various reasons. Pressuring or manipulating your partner to move prematurely to a higher level of commitment requires great sensitivity and tact, is risky, and often leads to frustration and disagreement. In this process, Smedes has said that the most common personal commitment mistakes are committing too quickly, not being mature enough to commit, being unable to communicate openly and having unrealistic expectations, low self-esteem, and unshared values. It can all get very complicated and cause a great deal of emotional suffering. Either partner can feel rejected and bewildered in the relationship if it does not move along as desired.

Managing New Relationships

Depending upon your attachment to past beliefs, you may now find it more or less difficult to adopt a new lifestyle that accommodates traditional morals and values with those of the post-1970 generation. Some people who are independent by nature or experience are literally afraid of making a new lifetime commitment. They may fear the possible economic responsibilities, the perceived restrictions on their social and professional lives, the threat of a new grief through divorce or death, or many other factors. Consequently, your new relationships may need to cycle through casual dating to monogamous dating several times before you finally find the person who will be appropriate for a full lifetime of sharing in marriage. You will need to learn how to manage your physical, intellectual, emotional and spiritual investment in a sexual friendship to avoid getting out of step with your partner and your own values.

Managing new relationships as you emerge from grief is a very sensitive and fragile process because your feelings are probably still very close to the surface and are easily stimulated, especially if your self-esteem is not yet completely reconstructed. The recovering bereaved person desperately needs patience, understanding and tolerance in the process of pair bonding because it is always a matter of reciprocal matching under conditions of high risk and uncertainty.

The pair-bonding process involves moving through the first stage of idealizing the loved one, through the second stage of confronting disillusionment as reality sets in and finally reaching a resolution or acceptance of humanness. Due to your possible attachment needs, you may find yourself involved in a harmful, painful relationship that you can neither break free of nor improve. Jed Diamond and Brenda Schaeffer described the difference between healthy love and unhealthy love. *Healthy love gets more comfortable and secure with time. Unhealthy or addictive love gets more painful and unstable with time.* Without professional help, you may be stuck in such a situation for months, or even years.

It might be assumed that mature adults can easily manage any disagreement or difference in values, likes and dislikes, misunderstandings, etc. Unfortunately, you may be acutely sensitive to any perceived threat to a new relationship, even an unhealthy one. Joan Atwood and Robert Chester called this reaction a variation of post-traumatic stress syndrome.

Your world which once seemed orderly and safe now may appear unpredictable and menacing. This feeling may derive from the fear of new grief should the relationship be terminated. It can literally thrust you backward into infantile behavior including fresh fears of abandonment based on lack of self-esteem and perceived insecurity. Any action by your partner which you perceive as negative, whether intentional or inadvertent, slight or significant, may trigger anxiety, illogical jealousy and even panic. It may create a defensive reaction to threat of new loss that is damaging to the relationship, possibly initiating the very terminal outcome that you fear. The suffering can be intense if one of the partners leaves and rejects a call for reunion in a one-sided relationship.

You may not yet be the secure, confident person you used to be. It will take time and work for you to know the new you and have confidence in your ability to be an effective, loving partner once again. New grief, despair and rage can result when only one partner in a romantic relationship has the complete experience of falling in love and the other responds only with companionship, or sexually without the pair bonding of genuine love. The one who is the more bonded can waver between euphoric bliss when the partner's behavior is positive to melancholy when it is not. The result can be a serial form of the proverbial lover's quarrels and reconciliations, with the cycle repeating itself indefinitely. A permanent break may only occur after a separation has lasted for a prolonged period, despite the suffering of the more smitten partner.

The key to this problem is open, nonjudgmental communication which permits negotiation of compromises that settle all your differences to the satisfaction of both partners. According to Sills, this process of negotiation is a natural stage in all romantic relationships and precedes the long-term unconditional commitment to each other that can lead to marriage. You can find just about any topic to fight about but the general themes of conflict among couples are identified as including money, sex, accountability, expectations, personal flaws, family and friends. At the center of these conflicts is the struggle for power — who is in control — and that makes us more interested in winning than in finding a compromise solution. Learning how to negotiate successfully is an important skill in building abiding relationships.

Character Traits Under Stress

David Viscott identified three different primary character traits among people that help explain their behavior under stress in intimate relationships. It would be good to understand these traits before beginning any new serious, intimate relationship. His three main character types are dependent, controlling and competitive.

Dependent people are warm and loving. Their bonding capacity is as strong as their self-esteem is weak. They quickly become attached to anyone who shows them affection so they are inclined to attach themselves to people indiscriminately. Their loving seems motivated by their need to be loved in return. They tend to hold on because they feel that having anyone is better than being alone. They try, but often fail, to earn love through their good deeds which may mask attempts to manipulate through indebtedness. Dependent people need to become more independent but such growth is often seen as betrayal by partners who count on their weakness to make themselves appear strong by comparison.

Controlling people want to control others because they often feel their own lives are out of control. They fear abandonment. Any withdrawal of affection frightens controlling people deeply. They are too closed and proud to admit to any weaknesses. Controlling people insist on winning, being right, having the last word, making the other person wrong and appearing blameless. They take criticism poorly. They tend to bear grudges and they cannot risk rejection. They consider obedience the best proof of love. Controlling people never feel close because they do not allow themselves to be vulnerable. They are often cold and give very little evidence of affection. They may isolate themselves from their feelings so they cannot be hurt.

Competitive people are always trying to prove they are better than others. Their self-esteem is very tentative, as each new venture contains the possibility of success or failure. They often work for the esteem and adoration of others. They can use their sexuality as a commodity, demanding that partners shower them with approval, gifts and compliments. They do not like to have their sincerity questioned and are deeply sensitive to being embarrassed. In their terms, love is praising them.

Since emotional maturity is a matter of relative degree that varies with individuals and develops with age and experience, everyone has some dependent, controlling and competitive traits. One style usually dominates our behavior under conflict or stress. Dependent, controlling and competitive people all seek to satisfy emotional needs in a relationship, but in different ways. Viscott explained how the interactions of these character types occur in the various possible combinations: dependent-dependent, dependent-controlling, dependent-competitive, controlling-controlling, controlling-competitive and competitive-competitive.

The object is not to change, but to be honest in dealing with your emotions with your partner. Understanding your style and how it interacts with that of your partner will help you have more effective communication and allow you to accept and support each other more completely. Unresolved grievances can fester and erode any relationship if they are not openly dealt with. Understanding how you react to such events is the first step to their solution.

Resolving Conflicts

No matter what character style you or your partner fall into when stressed, it is possible to have a loving, lasting relationship if you understand and accept your differences and reinforce each other's needs. Loving gives us courage to be our best and inspires us to realize our potential. With unconditional love a dependent person can become more independent, a controlling person can become less controlling. Movement in these more positive directions is a sign of a maturing personality.

Viscott also identified and explained the several different modes couples use in resolving conflicts. A happy couple and an unhappy couple have similar problems, they just solve them differently. There is conflict in every relationship, but *how* you fight is more important to the survival of the relationship than what you fight about.

Viscott offers the following emotional bill of rights:

Guidelines To A Healthy Relationship

Each partner has the right to express what he or she feels or thinks.
Each partner has the right to tell the truth.
Each partner has the right to be trusted and believed.
Each partner has the right to be listened to and to be understood.
Each partner has the right to admit weakness without being ridiculed.
Each partner has the right to express his or her needs and desires and to
   be taken seriously.

Each partner has the right to be heard in the context of the moment without being reminded of the past.
Each partner has the right to grow.
Each partner has the right to seek help, friendship and support.
Each partner has the right to be forgiven.

None of us is a perfect human being, so we can occasionally be expected to fail our partners or treat them unfairly. Whatever the form of your new intimate relationship, it is likely that from time to time your partner will do something that you experience as hurtful. Unresolved, these hurts can lead to rejection and hatred, according to Smedes. The realization that we cannot control the feelings or behavior of others, only our own, can be very painful if we have made a significant emotional investment in a relationship.

Smedes says that when you can settle an issue, forgive and go on, you again begin healing. That leads to recommitment and possibly an even stronger pair bonding. Reunion occurs within a boundary of new reality and the resulting pair bonding can be even more strengthened. This is what a healthy relationship is all about: trusting enough to allow feelings to be expressed openly, put in proper perspective, resolved directly and let go.

Forgiving is not tolerating unresolved grievances. To love someone unconditionally is the goal to work toward in any relationship. But sometimes you must stand up for what you believe to be moral and right in the circumstances. Sometimes goals can collide with the behavior of your partner. Either you choose to make your love for the relationship more important than what you believe to be right — or you choose to make your beliefs more important than the relationship. It's not being right or wrong, it is a choice based on what you believe is best in the long run.

If the painful behavior of your partner is not acknowledged and modified after you have made every effort to communicate your feelings, you have every right, possibly the obligation, to consider leaving the relationship. If in reality you are enduring real pain and suffering through disrespect, neglect, indifference, being deprived or exploited, then your feelings of rejection may be a valid reading of the situation.

Leman says that to continually suppress rage and humiliation is as bad for you as swallowing poison. Unfortunately, your feelings also may be invalid, based on faulty thinking and reflecting your own poor self-image and lack of self-esteem. So your feelings must be carefully tested against reality to avoid acting precipitously in response to your own insecurity. Unjustly or mistakenly accusing

your partner of an intolerable grievance out of your own insecurity
or jealousy may cause a breakup where none was intended. But
only you can make this determination, based on your values and
options and the risks involved. Counseling may be helpful in sort-
ing out reality from fantasy.

Ending A Relationship

While true platonic friendships can last a lifetime, be prepared for
the possibility that any love affair at this time may eventually break
up. There is a chance that whatever you experience during this
period of recovery will be viewed as a transitional experience when
you look back on it. If a relationship is ending, you might find it
useful to know that Pogrebin divided the process of termination
into three different styles: "baroque" endings, "classical" endings
and "romantic" endings. Baroque endings are accompanied by agi-
tation, accusations, flaming exit speeches, slammed doors and broken pottery. Classical endings include more rational, lucid, dignified
and calm exit behaviors, possibly after several attempts at reconciliation. Romantic endings are slower fadeouts, usually because the
cause of the ending may be less specific or too distressing to confront as one partner or the other gradually drifts away.

When the breakup of a love affair occurs, whether due to the
unparallel growth of the partners, boredom, jealousy, betrayal,
deadlock or some other flash point, you may experience some of
the same feelings you felt when your spouse died. Almost everyone
goes through a predictable series of emotional reactions, according to Stephen Gullo and Connie Church. First is a state of numbness and shock, disorientation and depression, followed by resignation, rebuilding and resolution. This process can take six months
and longer, depending upon your degree of attachment and emotional investment. No two people will experience these reactions
in the same way, due to the variety of their emotional investment
in the relationship. Although you experience them, you must continue to maintain your emotional center and go through your
daily routines while the love wounds heal. You may only recover
when sufficient time has lapsed to permit the onset of a new
relationship with another partner.

To be realistic, it may be necessary for you to experience several
such transitional connections and breakups on your way to a new
lifetime committed relationship, if that is the direction in which you
are heading. Although relationships can stabilize at any level of com-

mitment so long as both partners are content with the situation, it seems that romantic relationships either proceed toward commitment or else they recede toward breakup if either partner is not satisfied. Along the way both partners are likely to make some mistakes of action or judgment which hurt the other. If they are not forgiven, these hurts can add up and cause serious doubts about continuing.

If you are involved in a breakup, try to part as friends, with good wishes for the future happiness of your departed partner. Do not despair and try to not take it personally, although managing the inevitable mini-grief that results will demand great courage and energy. Try to consider it as a transitional learning experience. Try to identify what went wrong and seek to avoid repeating any mistakes you may have made. Forgive yourself for not being perfect, experience the pain of separation, pick yourself up and start again or reconcile yourself to being alone. Some counselors suggest a six-month withdrawal period while you reconstruct your self-image and redevelop your sense of wholeness.

Obviously, this is much easier and simpler to say than it is to do. It is a difficult transition and the necessity to confront such crises can remind you of the idealized relationship with your deceased spouse that you lost. It can retrigger the simmering grief all over again.

According to Halpern, no adult relationship can match marriage. However, your situation may or may not naturally encourage a new marriage. And to be realistic, the older you are, the stronger odds are against it, especially for women. The odds for men may be somewhat better because men tend to die younger, leaving more single, still active women than men in our society.

The commitment to be with another person again, sharing experiences and responsibilities in mutual caring, affection and support, is appealing. Now that you know what it is to lose such a relationship and now that you have made some adjustment to the loss, you may be wary of entering into such a relationship again.

To Remarry Or To Wait?

Even if you are willing to take the risks involved in loving again, there is one other thing to consider very carefully. If your personal growth and recovery from grief would be stifled, then a remarriage at this time would be premature. Perhaps a union should be postponed for a time to permit yourself to regain a stable, secure identity as a single person before you again give yourself in full commitment to another.

Before you seek remarriage, it may be desirable to work out your healing through a series of less committed transitional friendships, consistent with your values and religious views. Marriage later in life is much more complex than first marriages. Experienced partners bring a whole lifetime of wants, needs, wishes, desires, dreams, likes and dislikes into a mid-life marriage.

If you decide to remarry, Richard Stuart and Barbara Jacobson describe all the issues that should be settled in order to make a second marriage last and be happy. These issues include:

- Coming to terms with the positive and negative aspects of the first marriage
- Criteria for selecting a new mate (love may no longer be a sufficient reason for getting married, although most of us consider it to be desirable)
- Uncovering and negotiating "secret contracts" in the relationship (expectations that are not openly communicated)
- Managing separate estates and incomes
- Learning to really communicate and understand each other
- Resolving conflicts and making them work for the couple instead against them
- Balancing home life and work life (especially in two-career marriages)
- Resolving the status and roles of parenting with stepchildren and other relatives
- Establishing sexual loyalty and compatibility
- Developing the most enjoyable, exciting and enriching aspect of marriage, that of true intimacy.

And, of course, partners will want to know each other's background, recognize each other's likes and dislikes and know and share each other's ambitions, hopes and dreams. With all these issues demanding resolution, it should be clear that remarriage must be worked out carefully and deliberately the second time around.

Ironically, it seems that you are more likely to find a new love partner when you least feel the need for one. Survivors who seem to have the best chance of achieving success in new relationships are whole people. They have worked out their deepest emotional problems, they have found their new place in the world and they recognize that it takes a lifetime of work to maintain honest relationships. They are able to give the relationship the care it needs to survive because they have mastered their own survival and are no longer hoping romantic love or erotic attraction will save them. Many people who have come through periods of untimely grief have found other avenues for reconstruction, seeking companionship in community projects, family or even pets, after they developed good friendships and made strong commitments to their own development. They found new intimacy, not out of fear of being alone or out of need to addictively lose themselves in another, but out of the strength of their own new identity.

In this condition, they can set as a goal what Stephen Gullo and Connie Church call a synergistic form of love, one in which both people become greater than either one could become alone. Love synergy is an ideal worth striving for. But there are no guarantees and you must maintain reasonable expectations; even the best relationships require constant compromises and trade-offs.

Once people are honest with themselves, they can be honest with each other concerning their needs, strengths and weaknesses, admitting to each other their need for deliberate support to avoid regressing to obsolete roles. According to Becker, women should guard against abandoning their needs, work or friendships in order to assume a new caretaking role and men must avoid their tendency to control and dominate. Women should remain independent, and men should work toward more interdependence. The more capable you are of facing your own separateness and the more you can experience a mature sense of who you really are, the more dynamic a contribution you will be able to make to any new relationship.

From now on, no matter what kind of new relationships you may form, you will live with the knowledge that each time you separate from your friend, partner or spouse, it may be the last time. That fact alone can motivate you to make the best use of the time you have together because the only time you have for certain is now. So try to live happily in the present time and place, wherever it may be.

You may now want to turn to page 177 for a few final thoughts about grief as a family concern. However, for some of you the next chapter may be crucial to your complete recovery from your loss. *For those raised in dysfunctional families, or for those living in a dysfunctional family at the time of the loss, the grieving process can be much more complex.* Growth through grief and the creation of healthy new relationships will require attention to the concerns we discuss in the following section on "Loss and Dysfunctional Families."

Loss And Dysfunctional Families

If you read many magazine articles and/or books, you probably have noticed more and more these days words like "addiction," "dependency," "co-dependent" and "dysfunctional." From time to time we made such references as we went through the 20-Step model of recovery from grief. There is an increasing awareness in recent years of the impact of growing up in a dysfunctional family, one often made dysfunctional by addiction to alcohol and other drugs.

When loss comes to a person who was raised in a dysfunctional family, or who at the time of the loss lives in a dysfunctional family, recovery from grief is even more complicated and difficult. Every situation of grief is unique to the person who experiences it but there are some particular ways in which grief is likely to affect persons who have been raised in dysfunctional homes.

In this chapter we want to pay particular attention to some of the ways that growing up in a dysfunctional home could affect the way a person responds to a loss, such as the loss of a spouse later in life. To do this, we are going to reconsider our 20 Step model from the perspective of a person who had at least one alcoholic parent or who grew up in a home that was dysfunctional for another reason. Janet Geringer Woititz, Ed.D., an expert in this field, wrote a book entitled *Adult Children of Alcoholics* in which she suggested that Adult Children of Alcoholics (ACoAs) share certain characteristics with each other. After the publication of her work, Dr. Woititz became aware of the fact that some of the characteristics of ACoAs were shared by those raised in other types of dysfunctional families. She noted that even "if you did not grow up with alcoholism, but lived, for example, with other compulsive behaviors such as gambling, drug abuse or overeating, experienced chronic illness, profound religious attitudes, were adopted, lived in foster care, or in other potentially dysfunctional systems, you may find that you identify with the characteristics. It appears that much of what is true for the children of alcoholics is also true for others, and that this under-standing can help reduce the isolation of countless persons who also thought they were 'different' because of their life experience."

We will use the term ACoA for the sake of simplicity. However, the following discussion is also intended to apply to those raised in dysfunctional families other than alcoholic families.

Woititz worked with many ACoAs and discovered that certain themes seemed to recur over and over again.

Woititz's ACoA Characteristics

1. ACoAs guess at what normal behavior is.
2. ACoAs have difficulty following a project through from be-ginning to end.
3. ACoAs lie when it would be just as easy to tell the truth.
4. ACoAs judge themselves without mercy.
5. ACoAs have difficulty having fun.
6. ACoAs take themselves very seriously.
7. ACoAs have difficulty with intimate relationships.
8. ACoAs over-react to changes over which they have no control.
9. ACoAs constantly seek approval and affirmation.
10. ACoAs usually feel that they are different from other people.
11. ACoAs are super responsible or super irresponsible.
12. ACoAs are extremely loyal, even in the face of evidence that the loyalty is undeserved.

13. ACoAs are impulsive. They tend to lock themselves into a course of action without giving serious consideration to alternative behaviors or possible consequences. This impulsiveness leads to confusion, self-loathing and loss of control over their environment. In addition, they spend an excessive amount of energy cleaning up the mess.

It takes Dr. Woititz the space of a book to define and discuss each of these characteristics of the ACoA, something we obviously cannot do in this chapter. We can, however, expand a little on what she says about these characteristics, especially since each one may affect the way an ACoA manages grief.

In order to show the relationship of the 20 steps of grief and individual personality differences to a special life history or situation, we will discuss each of Woititz's 13 characteristics in terms of her understanding of ACoAs and also from the perspective of our 20 step model.

The following is based on the research reported in *Adult Children of Alcoholics.*

ACoAs Guess At What Normal Behavior Is

Dr. Woititz says that "the significance of this statement cannot be overestimated" as it is the "most profound characteristic of the Adult Child of an Alcoholic." ACoAs "simply have no experience with what is normal."

Being raised in a dysfunctional home is different from being raised in a healthy family, so the way the ACoA experiences early life provides fewer guidelines for how "normal" people relate or communicate or even how "normal" people feel. Of course, there may be no such thing as "normal" but the person raised in a dysfunctional home correctly intuits that something is wrong in the home even if no one actually says so. ACoAs typically think the something "wrong" is probably themselves. A lot of self-doubt is generated by being in a situation where family life is turned upside down. When something needs to be expressed, it may be overexpressed or more likely, underexpressed. Feelings can feel dangerous and better off hidden.

In the Feeling phase of the 20-Step model of grief, a person who grew up in an alcoholic or other dysfunctional home may have a harder time than others handling the emotional impact of the loss. Just as they did when they were children, they are prone to think they need to be strong and not let their feelings be known. When asked how they are doing, their difficulty in knowing what is normal to think or feel may lead them to hide their thoughts and feelings so as not to appear any more different than they have always felt they were.

This can create particular tension if the ACoA has the personality preferences of an Extravert and/or Feeling type. The Extravert has a natural tendency to communicate thoughts and feelings out loud and the Feeling type is particularly oriented toward other people. The personality dynamics that call for expression therefore run counter to what was learned in early home life, probably leaving the ACoA more vulnerable to feelings of being cut off from others at a time when the need for others is stronger than ever.

If others want to help, they may consider initiating the conversation about thoughts and feelings by talking about what would be normal for *them* to be thinking and feeling if they had just experienced such a loss. That kind of self-disclosure can make it safer for the ACoA to share what is going on inside. If you are the ACoA who has gone through a loss and you need to talk but are afraid to do so for fear of not sounding normal, you might consider asking a close friend what he or she would be thinking and feeling if they had gone through what you have. You will probably find that what they say is very close to what you have been struggling with. Hearing it from another can give you a sense of safety in expressing those things out loud.

The point is that we humans are a combination of our history, our personality, our life experiences and our present situation. Anything that has significantly affected any one of these areas of our life will affect what we experience as a painful loss and how we manage the grief that goes along with that loss. Sensitive self-care and sensitive care for others experiencing grief require us to be aware of individual differences and special life circumstances that may make the grieving process more complex and wrenching. The 20-Step model, combined with an appreciation for personality differences and an awareness of life experiences, can help us understand either a personal loss or a helpful response to someone else who is buckling under such a load.

With these general principles in mind, we shall now turn to the other characteristics of ACoAs. We will take time only to make some of the connections that would be important to keep in mind for yourself or as you offer support to others.

ACoAs Have Difficulty Following A Project Through From Beginning To End

Children raised in alcoholic or dysfunctional homes are likely to see fewer ideas, projects or possibilities worked through from beginning to end. It stands to reason. Whatever is making the family dysfunctional is apt to interrupt the normal progression of communications and behaviors that are needed to move from start to finish. Sometimes, Dr. Woititz says, adults who have come from such dysfunctional homes think they have a problem (or someone else thinks they do) with procrastination. In truth, they simply failed to learn what they needed to know in order to complete the task.

When a loss is experienced, it is hard for anyone to stay with the grief process from beginning to end. Most people want to run, not walk "through the valley of the shadow of death." This understandable tendency of people wanting to get the grief over with, to short-circuit what they hate, may be underscored for those whose early life experiences have not taught them to follow things through from beginning to end.

If you came from an alcoholic or other dysfunctional home and now are trying to recover from grief, you probably do not connect your feelings with your earlier experiences as much as you do with the desire to get past the loss and get on with life. There may, however, be more of a connection between the past and the present than you think. It would need to be studied more to know for certain but it could be that those raised in dysfunctional homes are more inclined to substitute, as we described earlier in the 20-Step model. To the extent that this is true, the short-circuiting of the grief process by Substitution would get in the way of a healthy resolution to the grief in Reconstruction.

ACoAs Lie When It Would Be Just As Easy To Tell The Truth

Denial of the problem is the classic defense of the alcoholic, and denial pervades the dysfunctional family system that results from living with an alcoholic. Whatever the nature of the dysfunction, children from dysfunctional homes typically find themselves pretending everything is all right at home and in their lives. Being honest about their feelings, either with themselves or with others, does not come easily. Woititz quotes a young woman with an alcoholic mother and father as saying, "I can feel absolutely shattered inside and someone will ask me how I'm doing, and I'll say, 'Fine.' "

There is such a thing as *conscious* denial, which is what we use when we deny something about ourself that we know to be true. We may consciously deny something in order to present ourselves in a more favorable light, to protect someone else or for a number of other reasons. In a loss situation, someone who was raised in a dysfunctional home may continue the pattern of not letting other people really see the hurt and the pain. When asked if everything is okay, the most predictable response would be "Yes," regardless of what is going on inside. That old discomfort with letting others really know what is going on does not go away easily.

In addition, it is important to remember that denial as a defense mechanism goes far beyond conscious denial to *unconscious* denial. This occurs when even the person who has the thoughts or feelings is unaware of what they are. When denial in this sense is a part of one's growing up experience, add that to the genuine shock and denial that is a natural part of our human reaction to a major loss and we have the stage set for problems with the experience and expression of feelings.

If feelings must be worked through to move through the grief process normally, and those feelings are relatively inaccessible or inexpressible, the potential for difficulty increases. When all these dynamics are compounded in a person who has a natural personality preference for keeping feelings in, the situation is even more complicated. In any case where feelings or their expression seem to be blocked, but especially when that is in combination with a history of family dysfunction, a trained and skilled counselor who knows about the dynamics of dysfunctional family life may be very helpful.

ACoAs Judge Themselves Without Mercy

Along with the tendency to put on a good front and not let others know how things really were or how you felt about them, if you were the child of an alcoholic or grew up in another kind of dysfunctional home, you probably were pretty hard on yourself. Even though now you may realize that the problems within your home were not really caused by you, early on in life you probably received the message that nothing you did was good enough. It is a short step from there to the feeling that, if only you have been better or gone about things better, home life would have improved. This is the scenario that emerged from Woititz's research with children of alcoholics and it is one that therapists recognize as arising from families with other kinds of problems as well.

How might this history show up in your life if you were to lose a spouse or someone else very significant in your life? The self-criticism and self-blame that often accompany grief may be even stronger for those who have long taken upon themselves the responsibility for bad things happening around them.

Strong guilt feelings may haunt ACoAs over the hurts they inflicted on the person who died, including those that were never actually inflicted but were thought about. And it is quite possible that such self-blame will be more self-condemning and last longer than what other persons might experience. That is because these feelings are being fueled by early life experiences in addition to whatever is actually related to the present situation. It is a double dose of blame. If the person who died was a parent, there may be additional self-judgment if the relationship with the parent was never reconciled. Unfinished business always compounds grief and adults who grew up in dysfunctional families have more unfinished business than most other persons.

One of the ways to break this cycle of self-blame is to become a part of an ACoA group. Hearing the similar stories of others can help you see that the kinds of feelings you had as a child were not as much related to what you were doing as to what was going on in your home — most of which was out of your personal control. Those persons with a Feeling personality type preference may have an even harder time letting go of their guilt over relationships that were not harmonious. If a group experience is not adequate or not appealing to you, then some individual sessions with a trained counselor could help. It rarely helps someone who feels guilty to say, "You shouldn't feel guilty," but it can help to understand what lies behind that guilt and how to do something constructive with those feelings.

ACoAs Have Difficulty Having Fun
ACoAs Take Themselves Very Seriously

Both these characteristics of Adult Children of Alcoholics can affect the way a person will handle the task of detachment during the grieving process. Detachment requires an ability to step back from a situation enough to gain some new perspective on it. Humor represents such a step back but some people have a harder time than others gaining this distance.

Those raised in dysfunctional homes came to believe that life is, as Woititz says, "a very serious, angry business." Such children have had a lot of the "child" in them squeezed out in the serious press that comes from being concerned about how to survive from day to day. There is not a lot of room for spontaneity in such a situation. It's hard to let go long enough to be spontaneous when you are not quite sure if you dare let go.

Staying in control as much as you can because the world around you is always threatening to get out of control does not equip you to let go, as grievers eventually must. As we have seen in the 20-Step model, those who do not detach cannot move on toward Reconstruction. Yet the safety associated with holding on is hard to trade for the insecurity of what might happen if you don't. Since life is perceived as a very serious business the consequences of making a mistake appear to be very serious also.

There is no simple prescription for learning to see life in a healthier perspective. Persons raised in a dysfunctional home, who also have a natural personality preference for Introversion, may have an additional challenge. Introverts typically are not comfortable sharing their inner thoughts and feelings with others unless they know them well. They are not as likely to try out ideas or test feelings by talking about them openly and listening for feedback, as more extraverted persons often do. Getting some distance from oneself and one's situation requires looking at things from a variety of perspectives. Talking with others (and really listening to what they say) is one way to gain that distance.

ACoAs Have Difficulty With Intimate Relationships

Another characteristic of Adult Children of Alcoholics that affects both Detachment and Reconstruction is the difficulty they have in trying to establish an intimate relationship. The problem is that as children they learned intimacy is very risky business. To draw close meant all the more pain when sent away. To love was to experience rejection. Woititz says it succinctly: "The fear of being abandoned is a terrible fear they grow up with." When they do grow up, every relationship or potential relationship is charged with an urgency born of the fear that something will go wrong and they'll be sent away once more.

When a spouse dies, there may be an even keener sense of abandonment than others feel because the death may represent another time when a loved one came close and then pulled away.

Most persons who die would prefer to live. When the spouse of someone raised in a dysfunctional home dies, it may almost seem they consciously chose to abandon the one who is left behind. Any survivor can have this feeling but those who have early in life come to expect that to love is to be rejected may be even more vulnerable to these feelings.

In Reconstruction, where the task includes moving toward others with some degree of openness, there may well be a higher than helpful level of concern about being hurt again. To allow others to get close has come to mean getting hurt, so the temptation may be high to avoid that hurt by not allowing anyone to get close again.

ACoAs Over-react To Changes Over Which They Have No Control

The kind of over-reaction to change Woititz refers to is related to the feeling while growing up that things are out of control — or about to go out of control. Consequently, the "child" inside the adult reacts to change in that old frightened way, even though the present circumstances may be quite different from what they were then.

In a grief situation, such reactions may lead to depression or withdrawal. They may also be involved in markedly impulsive behavior such as drinking, the use of other drugs or getting involved in premature and ill-advised relationships. Each of these behaviors may represent a way to regain a sense of control, even though the behaviors themselves look very much out of control. It may almost seem that these persons are defiantly engaging in behaviors that assert their right to do what they want. This may not be far from what the behavior is really about.

In effect, such behaviors may represent an effort to protest to the world: "I'm in charge of my life and I'm proving it by choosing this way to live it!" Underneath such protests usually is a fear that control is slipping away, which is why the person has to prove he is in charge. Helpful friends will focus in on the message rather than on the behavior, although that may be hard to do.

From a personality perspective, we might anticipate that the Introverted would initially react to feeling out of control more with depression and withdrawal and the Extravert in more action-oriented ways. It also would be important to pay attention to the message that comes through actions or behaviors that are very *uncharacteristic* for that individual. When that happens in others or in ourselves it is always significant.

ACoAs Constantly Seek Approval And Affirmation

Lacking a consistent sense of being "okay" while growing up, those raised in a dysfunctional family seem always to be seeking affirmation. They have a hard time really feeling okay even when affirmed. This affects the way ACoAs go about their ordinary life but when something extraordinary happens, such as the death of a spouse, the needs intensify. Shaken by the loss, the tendency may well be to somehow make the boundaries more secure. Substituting for the lost relationship may be a way such a person chooses in order to feel "okay" again as soon as possible. Unfortunately, relationships motivated by such needs are likely to be escapes from the pain of grief rather than healthy reintegration and reconstruction. Therefore they are more likely to fail, which precipitates another loss experience.

ACoAs Usually Feel That They Are Different From Other People

Feeling different is something that is hard for those from dysfunctional families to shake, even after they become adults. When a loss occurs, particularly if it is an untimely loss, the sense of being different that almost everyone feels is even stronger, since it comes on top of the lifelong experience of feeling different.

When we feel different, we are also likely to feel more isolated. Whether during the early Feeling steps or later contemplating Detachment, a person with a dysfunctional family history may find it harder to know how he "should" be feeling or what things would be like if he were to let go. Certain personalities, such as the Feeling types, may compensate for these feelings by focusing outward rather than inward, trying to make sure that other people feel comfortable when they are visiting during the grieving process. In that way, no one gets close enough to learn just how different the grieving person feels. Of course, the consequence is that the isolation is not broken into either.

ACoAs Are Super Responsible Or Super Irresponsible

During the grieving process, super irresponsibility is likely to stand out more than super responsibility. Yet being super responsible is no less a problem. Super responsibility as a personal characteristic growing out of a dysfunctional early home life is a way of dealing with underlying feelings of incompetence and feelings of not measuring up. The safer thing to do is not to let anyone know about that inner imperfection. Somehow or other ACoAs are convinced that imperfection and rejection are related. The more perfect the person the less likely that person will be rejected. The task is to keep others from discovering you aren't perfect. Woititz sees this as lying behind the ACoAs never wanting to say "no" and working hard to meet everybody else's needs, whatever the cost to themselves.

Such a person in the grief process may desperately want to keep up the appearance of being on top of the situation by going back to work and other activities right away, taking on more projects and generally handling the loss so well (perfectly) that others are amazed and impressed. What is not so obvious is that such behaviors may be coming out of great insecurity and inner feelings of inadequacy. From a religious perspective, it is an inner feeling of the Law rather than of Grace: If I do not do this, then something terrible (punishment) will happen.

Persons with certain personality type preferences may tend toward what is perceived as super responsibility. For example, the combination of Sensing and Judging (SJ) is often seen as a personality combination that holds to traditional values of work, family, religion and country. Persons with those personality preferences and with dysfunctional early life experiences might be even more likely to deal with grief by pouring themselves into activity, especially if Extraverts. It is also possible that friends who have those SJ preferences would be more likely to notice and affirm a grieving person's efforts to get back into the mainstream of normal, productive life.

What is of critical importance is that such a return to life and work come out of strength rather than being a compensation for inner feelings of not being okay and not wanting anyone else to know. Affirming the person rather than what the person is doing is the primary gift a friend can bring to someone dealing with grief in this way.

ACoAs Are Extremely Loyal, Even In The Face Of Evidence That The Loyalty Is Undeserved

During detachment, the letting-go process can be complicated by feeling disloyal if one does detach. There is also a sense of security that is maintained by holding on. The person who was raised in a dysfunctional home is more likely to have difficulty differentiating between what is truly loyal behavior and what arises out of fear and insecurity. The known represents more safety than the unknown and that fear gets confused with loyalty.

Feeling, Detachment and Reconstruction during the grieving process can all be affected by such loyalty. For example, wanting to make sure that the spouse or other person who was lost will be seen only in a good light may limit the expression of feelings, may make Detachment more difficult and may inhibit Reconstruction. Even though the spouse or other significant person has died, there is a certain security in maintaining that relationship. There is nothing wrong with this if it arises out of strength and conviction. However, if it is an expression of old fears and anxieties, then it is not life-serving and can get in the way of reintegration after a loss.

ACoAs Are Impulsive. They Tend To Lock Themselves Into A Course Of Action Without Giving Serious Consideration To Alternative Behaviors Or Possible Consequences. This Leads To Confusion, Self-Loathing And Loss Of Control Over Their Environment. In Addition, They Spend An Excessive Amount Of Energy Cleaning Up The Mess.

There are two primary ways in which this characteristic could be a factor in the recovery from grief. The more obvious one is when a person has such tendencies and is more likely to get caught up in self-destructive behaviors and relationships than others without such a family history. The sense of urgency that Woititz associates with the ACoAs, the feeling that if it is not done immediately there will be no second chance, lends itself to impulsive, ill-considered actions that have a high probability of turning out poorly. Poor Substitutions, premature Detachment and all that we earlier associated with "running through the valley" would be typical of those who are acting out this characteristic during the grief process. As we have seen, certain personality preferences may move in the direction of action rather than reflection, so when that is added to the dynamics that come out of early life experiences the tendency toward quick action may be even stronger.

The less obvious way ACoAs may be affected by a tendency toward impulsiveness is when, prior to the loss, they have experienced some of the consequences of such impulsive behavior. Those experiences may have been so destructive that the last thing they would want to do now in their grief is to add that kind of pain to what they are already experiencing. Consequently, they may feel afraid to do anything at all, to the point of feeling immobilized, as a defense against a natural tendency toward impulsive actions. Such rigidity is no more constructive in managing grief than impulsiveness — although the chances of hurting others along with oneself may be lessened. In both cases, what underlies the inner urge to impulsive action needs to be addressed. Probably talking with someone who understands these dynamics is the kindest thing we could do for ourselves or offer to another in this situation.

We have now completed our review of what Janet Woititz presents as the 13 primary characteristics of Adult Children of Alcoholics or others who came from dysfunctional homes. By taking these characteristics and rethinking them in the light of the 20-Step model and personality preferences, we suggest the management of grief will be even more effective if we take an individual's life history into consideration along with the present situation and personal strengths and limitations.

We also need to remember that sometimes people repeat their history in unfortunate ways which can further complicate the grief process. For example, it is not unusual for the child of an alcoholic to grow up and marry someone who has a problem with alcohol. If that happens, then the experiences while growing up are not just built-in memories, they may have continued as present realities. When a child of an alcoholic marries and then the alcoholic spouse dies, the grief process becomes incredibly more complex unless the survivor had already become involved in Al-Anon or had other help to understand his or her own co-dependent behavior.

The good news is that while we are affected by our past, we do not need to remain unduly controlled by that past. The marvelous capacity of human beings to choose is a constant reminder that change is possible. It is a further mark of grace that whatever the nature of our choices in the past, still this day there is the invitation — and the possibility — to choose life. The real purpose of our presentation of the 20-Step model is to help those individuals more consciously and consistently make those choices for life.

Managing Grief Is A Family Concern

Our focus in this book has been on you as a grieving spouse. We want to encourage you, as soon as you are able, to also help your family and friends to grieve. All those who loved D _____, children, brothers and sisters, parents and other close relatives and friends, must also grieve for their loss. As you could see when we were discussing dysfunctional families, every family is a complex social system. Dysfunction makes the family even more complex but even in the healthiest of families the management of grief is an intricate family concern. This is true whether or not all the family members are living in the same location because whether living near or far away, every family member will still experience some of the disruption to the family system that the loss of one of its members creates.

If your spouse died after a long illness, you are likely to be drained emotionally, spiritually, physically and mentally. There is scarcely any energy left for your own grief, let alone for supporting anyone else. Yet you as the spouse of the deceased may be seen as the key to the task oriented process of Acknowledgment, Feeling, Substitution, Detachment and Reconstruction. Family members will look for someone to take on the role of the deceased member of the family in their lives. You may be expected to take on that role along with your own. Understanding the 20-Steps of grief model may be one of the things you can offer that could be of benefit to the rest of the family. Introduce them to the model and encourage them to talk about their grief process as they experience it.

Do not be surprised if family members and friends have difficulty grieving. Unfortunately, as with the rest of us, probably nothing in their experience has adequately prepared them for grieving their loss. Society has a strange way of telling its children about life. The losses of pets or possessions are often lightly passed over with admonitions to avoid the symptoms of grief and to quickly replace the lost object with a substitute. "Don't cry, we will get you another one." Although some experience of natural death may be observed in school through changes of the seasons or the death of animals, adult human death is seldom talked about in the public schools. The denial of death is strongest when it comes to real, individual, personal loss. Unfortunately, we are keeping our children from understanding life when we deal with death in this way. Rather than trying to protect them from life, we should help them grow strong so they can deal with it. Now that a death has occurred in the family, they *must* deal with their loss, prepared or not. After you learn how to manage your own grief, you can be a great comforter and caregiver as you take on the role of wounded healer.

Especially if you have children at home, we think you should know something about family systems theory. When there is a loss of a family member, the entire family structure is changed. Nothing is exactly as it was before. If grief work is not completed by all members of the family, the reshaping is faulty and there will always be a hole in the family structure, left by the departed member.

Even though young children may not understand the full impact of the change, they are sensitive to a threat to their security. Although they may not be able to express their feelings well, they should be encouraged to grieve. If they don't experience the process for themselves, a loss later in life could trigger the unresolved grief process related to this loss and double their suffering later on. Adult siblings also need to work their way through grief to find a new equilibrium in their lives. They may also need to deal with unfinished grief work from earlier losses of their own that now get loaded onto the present loss of a mother or father. As the wounded healer in your family, you may be able to help them through their journey and in helping them, you may also help yourself.

Finally, *we believe that our model of grief applies not only to loss by death but also to other significant losses that people must face.* A crippling accident, a life-altering heart attack or other disabling illness, divorce or a drastic change in any important relationship — all of these losses can be devastating to people and lead to overwhelming feelings of grief. We are currently exploring the similarities and differences in these loss situations so we can see where the model fits well and where modifications need to be made. It may be that you know of someone who has not experienced a loss like yours but whom you recognize is clearly going through a grieving process. If our model has been of some help to you, perhaps it can be of some help to that individual also. We hope so.

Centuries ago, someone who knew what it was to walk some very dark and frightening paths said some words that we mentioned earlier because the world still remembers them: "Yea, though I walk through the valley of the shadow of death, I fear no evil — for You are with me" (Psalm 23). Though people still must walk through shadowed valleys, we believe this promise of presence continues to be kept. One of the ways we believe this promise is fulfilled is through the presence of caring family and friends. We have experienced for ourselves how others have been with us or entered into our lives at the greatest point of need. Now, through our model of grief, we hope to have passed a little of what we have received on to you.

Once again we suggest you seek professional help to work through your grief if it appears the steps of grief as briefly discussed in this book are beyond your ability to cope with them. Untimely grief is a natural response to untimely loss. Although it may make your life seemingly unbearable for a long time, you can eventually work through the challenges and emerge into life once more. It won't be

the same life, but it can be a good life. Although untimely grief
represents an untimely ending, it can also represent a new beginning.
May you be blessed in your search for healing and wholeness.

Afterword

A Final Word From Lew

I read many books but the ones that follow are those Dr. Gary Harbaugh and I found to be the most helpful in preparing this work. I extend my appreciation to all of these authors for their contribution to my own process of grief work. I encourage you to make continual use of these resources as I do. A useful personal library may be compiled from the books marked with an asterisk (*) after the title. Of course, you may get something different from them because we all learn what we need. In any case, I hope these books will become a working library for you as they have for me.

Finally, I want to leave you with the words of my father, as he lay in the nursing home during his last days, "I did the best that I could . . ." I have done my best to offer you in this book something out of my experience that I hope will help you also to do the best you can with the rest of your life.

A Final Word From Gary

In reading any book or using any resource, it is wise to remember that not everything written or said applies to every individual in the same way. Authors can only speak from their own experiences and resources. We not only have different personalities, we also have unique life histories and life situations. There is also a time when we are ready to hear things we might not have been able to hear earlier. The books we identify are ones that have been helpful in one way or another to us, but you may find that a book or resource we have not listed is the one that helps you the most. We would be glad to learn of such additional resources.

If you have found the MBTI to be helpful, write for more information to the Center for Psychological Type, 2720 N.W. 6th Street, Gainesville, Florida 32609, for more information and a catalog of resources. If you are looking for someone in your area who is a member of APT, write to The Association for Psychological Type, P.O. Box 5099, Gainesville, Florida 32602. Be sure that a person has been appropriately trained before allowing him or her to adminster and interpret the MBTI for you.

When it comes to professional help, which we have recommended at several points in our book, we encourage you to request the names of qualified persons from the various professional associations. Some of those are the American Psychological Association, the American Psychiatric Association, the National Association of Social Workers and the American Association of Pastoral Counselors. Members of each of these disciplines are trained differently so you might find one or another to be more appropriate for your need. Do not hesitate to ask a professional what training and experience she or he has had in grief work. If you come from a dysfunctional family, ask the therapist or counselor what their training is in family systems therapy or what they know about working with alcoholics or Adult Children of Alcoholics. Ethics require professionals to offer services only in their areas of competency. Each of the professional associations has regional or state offices which may offer referral resources.

Of course, ministers, rabbis and other religious leaders are among those most familiar with resource groups or professionals specializing in grief work. Even if you are not religiously inclined, you might inquire about professionals or support groups that have a good reputation for providing ethical and helpful guidance.

Funeral directors can also be a helpful source of information. An increasing number of funeral directors are sensitive to the counseling issues that arise when a death occurs and, if they do not offer support directly, they usually know what is available. Ask.

If you have a hospice in your area, the staff may be able to identify local professionals who have experience working with persons in grief situations. In addition, many local governments have agencies related to mental health that can recommend or conduct programs that might be helpful.

Most communities have Alcoholism Councils which provide referrals to individuals and groups working with persons and families affected by alcohol or other drug-related problems. If you have no such council in your community, AA and Al-Anon groups may know of such people or there may be an Adult Children of Alcoholics group or a Co-dependents Anonymous group somewhere in your vicinity. If you cannot locate one, you might try to contact the national headquarters of Co-dependents Anonymous, P.O. Box 33577, Phoenix, Arizona 85067 — or call (602) 944-0141. Of course, such groups are not a substitute for professional therapy. They are support groups, not therapy groups, but often members of such groups can identify professionals who have been of particular help to them.

The selection of a counselor who is qualified and who you believe truly understands you is very important. There are many different approaches to therapy, depending upon the profession and on the school where the professional was trained. Some offer individual therapy and some offer group therapy. You may find one or the other, or some combination of individual and group work, to be best for you. The therapist can help you decide.

You will want to feel that you can trust your therapist with your confidences. If you feel you cannot, then you need to talk that over with the therapist and then perhaps find another counselor. Before settling on a particular therapist, you could have an initial visit with several and then choose the one with whom you think you could accomplish the most. Although it may be upsetting at first to reveal your innermost feelings to a stranger, it is important to develop an open and honest relationship with your therapist as soon as possible. Holding back may prolong your healing and add to the time you need to be in treatment. There may be times when sessions are painful as you begin to get in touch with thoughts and feelings you have buried for some time, but through such opening up the grief wound is lanced and real healing can take place. Discuss your progress openly with your therapist and set some goals or criteria for deciding when to end therapy.

It may take some time before you feel you are ready to go on alone, but eventually the time will come to leave therapy. This will take some planning because ending your relationship with your counselor may itself be a loss experience. So carefully plan the ending of your counseling with your counselor. Then put what you have learned to good practical use in your life. Do not be surprised if, somewhere along the line, you feel like returning to your counselor for a "booster" session. That can be a very constructive thing to do, so call if you feel it could help.

It is now time to share with you some fine reading resources. We hope our work has been of help to you, but our book is only one of many that has good ideas you may want to consider. Whether what you need comes primarily through our work, one of the books in this bibliography or through a counselor, Lew and I wish you only the best as you take the next steps along your personal path to healing and wholeness.

References

What follows is a list of books that were used in the research for our model of grief work. Other sources included interviews with grieving spouses in support groups, the instructions received from professional counselors and the lectures and interactions occurring at several grief workshops, including the "Life, Death, Transition" workshop conducted internationally by Dr. Elizabeth Kubler-Ross, and agencies/groups such as the Saint Francis Center, Parents Without Partners, Widowed Persons Service and THEOS (They Help Each Other Spiritually) Foundation. Information about the "Personality and the Perception of Loss" workshops of Dr. Gary L. Harbaugh, Ph.D., may be received by contacting him at Trinity Lutheran Seminary, 2199 E. Main Street, Columbus, Ohio 43209, phone (614) 235-4136.

The American Psychiatric Association, *Diagnostic and Statistical Manual of Mental Disorders* (3rd Ed., Rev.), Washington, D.C., 1987.

Anderson, Bernhard W., **Understanding the Old Testament,** 4th Ed. Prentice Hall, Englewood Cliffs, NJ, 1976.

The Augustine Fellowship, *Sex and Love Addicts Anonymous.* * The Augustine Fellowship, Sex and Love Addicts Anonymous, Fellowship-Wide Services, Inc., Boston, 1986.

Bachmann, Charles C., **Ministering to the Grief Sufferers.** Prentice Hall, Englewood Cliffs, NJ, 1964.

Backus, William, **Finding the Freedom of Self Control.** Bethany House Publishers, Minneapolis, MN.

Barlow, David H. and Cerny, Jerome A., **Psychological Treatment of Panic.** * The Guilford Press, NY, 1988.

Baum, Gregory, "Man in History. The Anthropology of Vatican II" in *The New Morality,* William Dunphy, ed. Herder and Herder, NY, 1967.

Beattie, Melody, **Beyond Co-dependency.** Harper & Row, NY, 1989.

Beck, Aaron T., **Cognitive Therapy of Depression.** The Guilford Press, NY, 1979.

Becker, Carol, The Invisible Drama. Macmillan, NY, 1987.

Boerstler, Richard W., **Letting Go: A Holistic and Meditative Approach to Living and Dying.** Associates in Thanatology, Watertown, MA, 1982.

Bowlby, John, **Attachment and Loss: Loss, Sadness, and Depression,** Vol. III. Basic Books, NY, 1980.

Bozarth-Campbell, Alla, **Life is Goodbye, Life is Hello.** * CompCare Publications, Minneapolis, MN, 1985.

Brown, L., **The Psychology of Religious Belief.** Academic Press, Orlando, FL, 1987.

Bruckner-Gordon, Fredda; Gangi, Barbara; Wallman, Geraldine, **Making Therapy Work.** Harper & Row, NY, 1988..

Burgess, Jane K., **The Single Again Man.** * D.C. Heath, Lexington, MA, 1988.

Burns, David D., **Feeling Good.** * NAL Penguin, NY, 1980.

Burns, David D., **Intimate Connections.** * NAL Penguin, NY, 1985.

Cabot, Tracy, **Man Power.** * St. Martin's Press, NY, 1988.

Campbell, Joseph, ed. **The Portable Jung.** Penguin Books, NY, 1985.

Campbell, Scott and Silverman, Phyllis, **Widower.** * Prentice Hall, Englewood Cliffs, NJ, 1987.

Carlson, Dwight L., **Overcoming Hurts and Anger.** * Harvest House, Eugene, OR, 1981.

Childs, James M., **Christian Anthropology and Ethics.** Fortress Press, Philadelphia, 1978.

Colton, Helen, **Touch Therapy.** * Kensington Publishing, NY, 1983.

Cullman, Oscar, "Immortality or Resurrection", in Krister Stendahl, ed., **Immortality and Resurrection**. Macmillan, NY, 1965.

Davidson, Glen, **Living with Dying**. Augsburg, Minneapolis, MN, 1975.

Davidson, Glen, **Understanding Mourning: A Guide For Those Who Grieve**. Augsburg, Minneapolis, MN, 1975.

DeHaan, M. R., **Coming Events in Prophecy**. Radio Bible Class, 1962.

Diamond, Jed, **Looking For Love In All The Wrong Places.*** G. P. Putnam's, NY, 1988.

Dyer, Wayne W., **Pulling Your Own Strings**. Avon Books, NY, 1978.

Emery, Gary, **Own Your Own Life.*** Signet NAL Books, NY, 1982.

Faucett, Robert and Carol Ann, **Personality and Spiritual Freedom**. Image Books, Doubleday, NY, 1987.

Frankl, Viktor, **Man's Search for Meaning**. Pocket Books, NY, 1963.

Freeman, Lucy, **Listening to the Inner Self**. Jason Aronson, NY, 1984.

Freud, Sigmund, **Mourning and Melancholia**, (1917) in collected papers, Basic Books, NY, 1957.

Fromm, Erich, **The Art of Loving**. Harper & Row, NY, 1956.

Glick, Ira O., Weiss, Robert S., Parkes, C. Murray, **The First Year of Bereavement**. Wiley, NY, 1974.

Goldberg, Herb, **The Hazards of Being Male.*** NAL Penguin Signet, NY, 1987.

Gottschalk, Louis A. **How to do Self-Analysis and Other Self-psychotherapies**. Northvale, NJ: Jason Aronson, 1987.

Graham, Billy, **Angels**. Doubleday, NY, 1975.

Grant, W. Harold, Thompson, Magdala and Clarke, Thomas, **From Image To Likeness: A Jungian Path In The Gospel Journey**. Paulist Press, NY, 1983.

Griest, John H. and Jefferson, James W., **Depression and Its Treatment**. Warner, NY, 1984.

Gullo, Stephen and Church, Connie, **Loveshock.*** Simon & Schuster, NY, 1988.

Hajcak, Frank, and Garwood, Patricia, **Hidden Bedroom Partners.*** Libra Publishers, San Diego, 1987.

Halpern, Howard M., **How to Break Your Addiction to a Person.*** Bantam Books, NY, 1982.

Hammer, Allen. "Psychological Type and Coping," presented at APT VIII, Boulder, CO: June, 1989.

Hammer, Allen and Marting, M. Susan, "Coping Resources Inventory," Consulting Psychologists Press, Palo Alto, CA, 1987.

Harbaugh, Gary L., "A Model for Caring" in *Thanatos,* Winter, 1983.

Harbaugh, Gary L., "Death and Identity: Implications for Pastoral Care" in Brian O'Conner, ed., *The Pastoral Role in Caring for the Dying and*

Bereaved, Praeger, NY, 1986 (based on *The Voice of the Dying,* University of Chicago, 1968).

Harbaugh, Gary L., **God's Gifted People,** Augsburg Publishing House, Minneapolis, MN, 1988.

Harbaugh, Gary L., **The Faith-Hardy Christian.** Augsburg, Minneapolis, MN, 1986.

Harbaugh, Gary L., **Pastor as Person,** Augsburg, Minneapolis, MN, 1984.

Harbaugh, Gary L., "Personality and the Perception of Loss" in *Library of Congress,* Washington, DC, 1986.

Harbaugh, Gary L., "Death: A Theological Reformulation of Developmental and Existential Perspectives," The University of Chicago: University Microfilms, 1973.

Hirsh, Sandra and Kummerow, Jean, **Lifetypes.** Warner Books, NY, 1989.

Holmes, T.H. and Rahe, R.H., "The Social Readjustment Rating Scale" in *Journal of Psychosomatic Research* 11 (April 1967): 213-218.

Hritzak, John. **The Silent Company: How to Deal with Loneliness.**

Jackson, Edgar N., **Understanding Grief.** Abingdon Press, NY, 1957.

James, John W. and Cherry, Frank, **The Grief Recovery Handbook.**＊ Harper & Row, NY, 1988.

Jampolsky, Gerald, **Love Is Letting Go of Fear,** Celestial Arts, Millbrae, CA, 1979.

Jeffers, Susan, **Feel the Fear And Do It Anyway,**＊ Harcourt Brace Jovanovich, San Diego, New York, London, 1987.

Johnson, Ben, "Biblical Perspective on Death and Dying", Convocation on Death Dying and Other Losses, Gary L. Harbaugh, Convener, Hamma School of Theology, 1978.

Jung, Carl G., **Psychological Types.** Princeton University Press, NJ, 1971.

Jung, Carl G., **Modern Man In Search of a Soul.** Harcourt Brace Jovanovich, NY, 1933.

Justice, Blair, **Who Gets Sick.**＊ Peak Press, Houston, TX, 1987.

Kamm, Phyllis and Weizman, Savine G., **About Mourning — Support and Guidance for the Bereaved.**＊ Human Sciences Press, NY, 1985.

Kantonen, T. A., **Life After Death.** Fortress Press, Philadelphia, 1962.

Kast, Verena A., **A Time to Mourn: Growing Through the Grief Process.** Daimon Verlag, Einsiedeln, Switzerland, 1988.

Keller, Helen. **The Story of My Life.** New York: Signet Classic, 1988.

Kiersey, David and Bates, Marilyn, **Please Understand Me.**＊ Prometheus Nemesis, Del Mar, CA, 1984.

Kubler-Ross, Elisabeth, **Death, The Final Stage of Growth.** Simon & Schuster, NY, 1975.

Kubler-Ross, Elisabeth, On Death and Dying.* Macmillan, NY, 1969.

Kummerow, Jean, "Talking in Type." Center for the Applications of Psychological Type, Gainesville, FL.

Kushner, Harold S., When Bad Things Happen to Good People. Schocken, NY, 1981.

Lauer, Robert H. and Lauer, Jeannette C., Watersheds — Mastering Life's Unpredictable Crises.* Little, Brown, Canada, 1988.

Le Haye, T., Spirit Controlled Temperament. Tyndale House, Wheaton, IL, 1966.

Leman, Kevin, The Pleasers.* Dell Publishing, NY, 1987.

Lewis, Clive S., A Grief Observed.* Bantam, NY, 1961.

Lindemann, Erich, Beyond Grief: Studies in Crisis Intervention. Jason Aronson, Northvale, NJ, 1979.

Lindsey, Hal, There's A New World Coming. Vision House, Santa Ana, CA, 1973.

Madow, Leo, Guilt — How to Recognize and Cope With It. Jason Aronson, Northvale, NJ, 1988.

Malone, Patrick T., and Malone, Thomas P., The Art of Intimacy.* Prentice Hall, Englewood Cliffs, NJ, 1987.

Maslow, Abraham. Motivation and Personality. NY: Harper, 1954.

Mason, M. and Merle, M., Facing Shame: Families in Recovery. Norton, NY, 1987.

May, Rollo, The Meaning Of Anxiety.* Simon and Schuster, NY, 1979.

May, Rollo, Love and Will. Dell, NY, 1969.

McCary, James and McCary, Stephen, McCary's Human Sexuality, 4th Ed., Wadsworth Publishing, Belmont, CA, 1982.

McConnell Adeline, and Anderson, Beverly, Single After Fifty,* McGraw-Hill, NY, 1978.

Mellody, Pia, Facing Co-dependence. Harper & Row, NY, 1989.

Meuser, Fred W., Luther the Preacher, Augsburg Publishing, Minneapolis, MN, 1983.

Money, John, Love and Love Sickness, Johns Hopkins University Press, 1980.

Moody, Raymond A., Life After Life.* Bantam, NY, 1975.

Myers-Briggs, Isabel B., Gifts Differing.* Consulting Psychologists Press, Palo Alto, CA, 1980.

Myers-Briggs, Isabel B., Introduction to Type.* Consulting Psychologists Press, Palo Alto, CA, 1987.

Ostenviess, Soloman, Green, Bereavement; Reactions, Consequences and Care.* National Academy Press, Washington, DC, 1984.

O'Neill, Nena and George, Shifting Gears. M. Evans, NY, 1974.

Parkes, Colin M., **Bereavement: Studies of Grief in Adult Life.** International Universities Press, NY, 1972.

Parkes, Colin M., **Recovery From Bereavement.*** Basic Books, NY, 1983.

Peck, M. Scott, **The Road Less Travelled.*** Touchstone, NY, 1978.

Peele, Stanton, **Love and Addiction.** Signet NAL Books, NY, 1975.

Phillips, D., **How to Fall Out of Love.** Houghton Mifflin, Boston, 1978.

Pines, Ayala M., **Keeping the Spark Alive.*** St. Marten's Press, NY, 1988.

Pogrebin, Letty Cottin, **Among Friends.*** McGraw-Hill, NY, 1987.

Quenk, A.T. and Quenk, Naomi, "The Use of Psychological Typology in Analysis," in M. Stein, ed., **Jungian Analysis.** Open Court Press, La Salle, IL, 1982.

Quenk, Alex T. **Psychological Types and Psychotherapy.** Gainesville, FL: Center for Applications of Psychological Type, 1985.

Quinnett, Paul G., **Suicide, the Forever Decision.*** Continuum Publishing, NY, 1987.

Rando, Therese A., **Loss and Anticipatory Grief.*** D.C. Heath, Lexington, MA, 1986.

Rhodes, Sonya and Potash, Marlin S., **Cold Feet — Why Men Don't Commit.*** E.P. Dutton/NAL Books, NY, 1988.

Ring, Kenneth, **Life at Death: A Scientific Investigation of Near-Death Experience.*** Quill, NY, 1982.

Rush, H. M. F., **Behavioral Theories and Theorists**, McGraw-Hill, NY, 1977.

Scarf, Maggie, **Intimate Partners.** Random House, NY, 1987.

Schaef, Anne Wilson, **Women's Reality.** Winston Press, Minneapolis, MN, 1981.

Schaeffer, Brenda, **Is It Love or Is It Addiction?** Hazelden, MN, 1989.

Schwarz, Hans, **Beyond the Gates of Death.** Augsburg Publishing, Minneapolis, MN, 1981.

Seilhamer, Frank H., **Here Am I: A Study of the Presence of God in the Old Testament and the Writings of Luther.** C.S.S. Publishing, Lima, OH, 1972.

Shahan, Lynn, **Living Alone and Liking It.*** Warner Books, Beverly Hills, CA, 1981.

Sharp, Daryl, **The Survival Papers.** Inner City Books, Toronto, 1988.

Siegel, Bernie S., **Love, Medicine & Miracles.*** Harper & Row, NY, 1986.

Sills, Judith, **A Fine Romance.*** Jeremy P. Tarcher, Los Angeles, 1987.

Silverman, Phyllis R., **Helping Each Other In Widowhood.*** Health Services, NY, 1973.

Singer, June, **Boundaries of the Soul: The Practice of Jung's Psychology.** Doubleday, NY, 1973.

Smalley, Gary and Trent, John, **The Blessing**. Thomas Nelson, Nashville, TN, 1986.

Smedes, Lewis B., **Forgive and Forget**. Simon & Schuster, NY, 1986.

Smedes, Lewis B., **Caring & Commitment: Learning to Live the Love We Promise**. Harper & Row, NY, 1988.

Stearns, Ann K., **Living Through Personal Crisis.** * Ballantine Books, NY, 1984.

Stein, Murray, **In Mid-Life: A Jungian Perspective.** * Center for Application of Psychological Type, Gainesville, FL, 1983.

Storr, Anthony, **Solitude, A Return to the Self**. Free Press, NY, 1988.

Stuart, Richard B. and Jacobson, Barbara, **Second Marriage. Make It Happy. Make It Last.** * Penguin Books, Canada, 1985.

Switzer, David, K., **The Dynamics of Grief**. Abingdon, Nashville, TN, 1970.

Tatelbaum, Judy, **Courage to Grieve: Creative Living, Recovery and Growth Through Grief**, Harper and Row, NY, 1980.

Viscott, David, **I Love You, Let's Work It Out,** * Simon & Schuster, NY, 1987.

Von Franz, Marie-Louise and Hillman, James, **Jung's Typology**. Spring Publications, Dallas, 1982.

Walters, Richard, **Sexual Friendships.** * Libra Publications, San Diego, 1988.

Wegner, Daniel M., **White Bears and Other Unwanted Thoughts**. Viking Press, NY, 1989.

Westheimer, Ruth and Lieberman, Louis, **Sex and Morality**. Harcourt Brace Jovanovich, Orlando, FL, 1988.

Whitfield, Charles L., **Healing the Child Within**. Health Communications, Pompano Beach, FL, 1987.

Wienhold, Barry K. and Wienhold, Janae B., **Breaking Free of the Co-dependency Trap**. Stillpoint Publishing, Walpole, MA, 1989.

Woititz, Janet G., **Adult Children of Alcoholics**. Health Communications, Pompano Beach, FL, 1983.

Wolfe, Thomas. **The Hills Beyond** New York: Harper, 1941.

Worden, I.W., **Grief Counseling and Grief Therapy.** * Springer, NY, 1982.

Yapko, Michael, D., **When Living Hurts.** * Brunnel/Mazel, NY, 1988.